Praise for *Casino Gambling the Smart Way!*

"A great book for the recreational gambler, or the player on a fixed income. A lot of great lessons, in a short-chapter, easy-to-follow style."

—Phil Hellmuth, Jr., winner of the 1989 World Series of Poker

"Glazer combines common sense, humor, and an insider's knowledge to help the lay gambler enjoy his dreams without getting swallowed whole by the dead-eyed sharks of casinoland."

—Wilcox Snellings, the world's number-one rated backgammon player

"A new and unconventional way to think about gambling, making it more fun and more profitable without hours of study. Glazer shows players how to break out of losing patterns and get a lot more bang for their gambling buck. Most readers will wish they'd read it before their last trip to Las Vegas!"

—Bob Kriegel, author of *Sacred Cows Make the Best Burgers* and *If It Ain't Broke, Break It!*

"I decry the gambling epidemic in America; too many people use gambling as a quick fix to ignore or cover over significant problems in their lives. But if someone is determined to gamble, following Andy Glazer's advice and approach will reduce the damage. *Casino Gambling the Smart Way* offers a funny, intellectually sound, psychologically valid approach to surviving the casino."

—George Leonard, author of *Mastery and The Ultimate Athlete*

"Glazer's engaging, irreverent book teaches anyone— even if you have trouble counting to ten—how to crack the casino's system. Derek Bok, the former head of Harvard University, once said that a college education is expensive, but less expensive than the alternative. Glazer delivers a first-rate education at a fraction of the cost of a bad run at craps or 21. If you can afford to subsidize casinos, don't buy this book. If you're tired of the dealer having the edge, buy it! Casinos are going to hate this book!"

—Adam Robinson, cofounder of The Princeton Review and author of numerous bestsellers, including *Cracking the SAT*

"A unique and valuable addition to gambling literature. Other gambling books aim too high, with complex mathematics, or too low, with empty truisms like 'know when to hold 'em and know when to fold 'em.' Andy Glazer has written the only book I've ever seen that actually offers practical advice for the purely recreational player. *Casino Gambling the Smart Way* is a winner!"

—Jake Jacobs, blackjack and backgammon professional, and author of *Can A Fish Taste Twice As Good* **and** *A Funny Thing Happened On The Way To The Four Point.*

"To his credit, Glazer doesn't offer up a miracle 'system' that will make us winners every time we sit down in a casino. There are two sure things here: Reading *Casino Gambling the Smart Way* will increase your chances of winning, and following Glazer's advice will ensure you enjoy yourself along the way."

—Paul B. Campbell, educator, former syndicated gambling columnist, and winner of four national sports media handicapping competitions.

Casino Gambling the Smart Way

How to Have More Fun and Win More Money

By
Andrew N. S. Glazer

CAREER PRESS

Franklin Lakes, NJ

CASINO GAMBLING THE SMART WAY
Cover design by Design Solutions
Typesetting by Eileen M. Munson
Printed in the U.S.A. by Book-mart Press

To order this title, please call toll-free 1-800-CAREER-1 (NJ and Canada: 201-848-0310) to order using VISA or Master Card, or for further information on books from Career Press.

The Career Press, Inc., 3 Tice Road, PO Box 687, Franklin Lakes, NJ 07417

Library of Congress Cataloging-in-Publication Data

Glazer, Andrew N. S.
   Casino gambling the smart way : how to have more fun and win more money / by Andrew N. S. Glazer.
     p.   cm.
   Includes index.
   ISBN 1-56414-416-X (pbk.)
     1. Gambling.   2. Casinos.   I. Title
GV1301.G53   1999
   795--dc21   98-49898

For
Milt Flack

**Philosopher, curmudgeon, mentor,
backgammon buddy, second father,
and a very dearly missed friend.**

Acknowledgments

"If I have seen further it is because I have stood on the shoulders of giants."

—Sir Isaac Newton

I don't know that I've seen further than anyone else, but however far I *have* seen is a direct result of the many people who, in teaching, supporting, and putting up with me, have lent me their literal or figurative shoulders. For me, Sir Isaac's quote means that we all build on the work of our teachers, and if my life had not been touched by so many good people, I wouldn't have had the skills or desire to write this book.

Some of the people I want to acknowledge most deeply won't be able to read this, at least not unless there is a decent-sized library in heaven:

My father, Edward L. Glazer, who marked me so strongly with his sense of decency, ethics, fairness, and pride in accomplishment, as well as his love. I was blessed to have 16 years with him, and 26 years later, I still yearn for more.

My second father, Milt Flack, to whom I dedicated this book, because of the inspiration he provided in teaching me to follow my own path. I wish you'd taken better care of yourself, you old pirate.

My good friend Dr. Frank Blaydes, taken from us in a plane crash at age 33, a great loss to the rural community he wanted to serve in a family medical practice, a funny, brilliant man, and a model of ethics and integrity to all his friends.

My good friend Lisa Heiszek, such a dear, kind, and gentle soul, so sensitive to the pain of others, and who felt too much pain herself to go on.

It has been so hard living without you. I think about each of you so often, and hope dearly that I can live up to the high standards each of you set. In my more ambitious moments, I find myself hoping I can carry on some part of the work each of you began. If by the time I'm done I can say that I gave the world even a small percentage of what any of you did, I will have lived a very good life indeed.

Fortunately, most of the people I want to acknowledge are still with us: My mother, Shirley Glazer Shafron, my sister, Donna Hall, and her husband, Ken, all of whom have given me unconditional love, and who are models of kindness and compassion. My friend Cornelia Cho, who set me on the path that led me to my new home and life. My teacher John Soper, who guided me through more difficult times than I can count. My Esalen boss Bill Herr, who led great writing groups and taught me how bosses can still be heartful friends. My writing buddy and soon-to-be screenplay superstar Steve Hayes, an even better person than he is a writer, and who believed in me as powerfully as I believe in him. My longtime close friend Bob Rasche, part of so many memories, a great architect, great athlete, great companion, and the second-best rotisserie player I know.

The steadfast Andy Palace, perhaps the most ethical person I know, who shares so many interests and has shared so much laughter with me. My brilliant and dear friend Howard Ring, part of more than a few memories himself, who has traded the student/teacher role back and forth with me for years. My irrepressible, funny, great pal from *Emory Law Times* days until now, poor old Jordan himself, the secretly heartful Downtown Kenny Brown. The uniquely wonderful techo-wizard hippie Michael Harris, with whom I share so many wavelengths. The kind, gentle, energetic, adventurous, and impossibly young Jim Adair, a philosopher beyond his years, and a special person and friend. You've all been there when I needed you, which has been often.

My buddy John Hoernemann deserves special notice too, for being my primary source of writing feedback, playing the role of the novice gambler. Like my one-act play *The Facilitator Strikes Back,* this book would not be as good, but for his input and suggestions.

My agent, Sheree Bykofsky, has been a big help and booster, and it seems only right that we got together as author and agent while living 3,000 miles apart, because (as we only found out after agreeing to work together) we lived six blocks apart as children. I'm not sure where my primary contact with The Career Press, Anne Brooks, grew up, but she makes me think that most author stories about nightmarish publishers stem mostly from artistic author temperaments. Working with Anne has been a pleasure, even when we disagree.

I started to name a great many more people, but the list quickly got out of control. I don't know if that happened because I'm so advanced in years (42, bless Douglas Adams) or because I lived and worked for two years in a very special place with a lot of very special people, The Esalen Institute, in Big Sur, California. Indeed, I probably never would have written this book, but for the inspiration that my first Esalen teacher, George Leonard, provided in his *Writing and the Act of Creation* workshop, a magical weekend that changed my life forever. But when the list got to 70, 80, 90 names and was still growing, I started to realize that listing everyone important from Esalen was an impossible task, let alone listing all the other friends, family, and teachers who have made a difference in my life. Paradoxically, the list was both too long, and not long enough; I was sure to forget someone.

So, with a couple of larger-than-life exceptions, I have not listed Esalen folks individually, and instead want to offer a acknowledgment to Esalen as an entity, for what it did to prepare me to write this book, and it goes out along with all my hopes for a speedy, relatively painless recovery from the battering El Niño handed it.

To all those Esalen people I started to name, and to all the other people who have helped me along the way; I love each of you, often in different ways, for the uniquely different combinations of love, friendship, and support you have given me, and for all the fun and adventures. I wrote this book to entertain and help people. If any of that happens, you each get a piece of the good karma. Because of all you've bestowed on me, there's plenty to go around.

Andy Glazer
Palo Alto, California
November, 1998

Contents

Introduction   15

Preface   21

Part One: Before You Leave for Las Vegas

Chapter 1
Float Like a Butterfly, Sting Like a Bee: 25
Play With the Style of Muhammed Ali

Chapter 2
Who Ya Tryin' to Impress?   29

Chapter 3
Gambling Vacations Are Not All Created Equal   33

Chapter 4
If You Bring $300 to Lose, You Will!   37

Chapter 5
Play It Cool When You Arrive,   41
and Your Bankroll Will Survive

Part Two: Gambling Systems and Other Bad Ideas

Chapter 6
The Not-So-Great Martingale Debate   47

Chapter 7
One-Hour (and Three-Year) Martinizing   51

Chapter 8
The Colonel Klink Theory of Decision-Making   55

Chapter 9
The Ultimate in Air Security   59

Part Three: Know Thyself

Chapter 10
The Basics: Food, Water, and Rationalizations   69

Chapter 11
Are You 90% Sure? 73

Chapter 12
$= MC^2$: Glazer's Theory of Relativity 79

Chapter 13
Ready, Fire, Aim! 85

Chapter 14
(Per)Cents and Sensibility 89

Chapter 15
Without Questions, There Are No Answers 93

Chapter 16
To Maintain Your Power, Don't Drive for an Hour 97

Part Four: A Winning Frame of Mind

Chapter 17
The Big Score, Part One: The Lottery 103

Chapter 18
The Big Score, Part Two: Realistic Longshots 107

Chapter 19
How Much Is the Free Lunch Today? 113

Chapter 20
Are You a TEF Guy? 117

Chapter 21
The Only Game in Town 121

Chapter 22
Easy Come, Easy Go? NO, NO, NO! 125

Chapter 23
The Champion's Choice: Intuition or Logic? 131

Part Five: Advice for Specific Games and Situations

Chapter 24
One-Armed Bandits and   137
Their Two-Legged Customers

Chapter 25
Video Poker and Other Smart Slot Machine Plays   141

Chapter 26
It's Not Polite to Point at a Slot Machine...   147
Unless It's With Your Pinky

Chapter 27
The Gambler's Ultimate Weapon   151

Chapter 28
Blackjack (and Airline Piloting) Made Simple   155

Chapter 29
The Three Ways to Win   159

Chapter 30
Picking the Right Opponents   165

Chapter 31
Say, Is This Here an Honest Game?   171

Chapter 32
Coppers and Robbers   175

Chapter 33
The Sucker's Only Even Break   181

Chapter 34
Taking a Shot at Low Risk: 185
The Casino Tournament

Chapter 35
Table Games: *The Next Generation*   191

Chapter 36
   Sports Betting, Swamp Land,   195
   and Other Good Investments

Part Six: Closing Thoughts

Chapter 37
   Andy's Enlightened Casino: A Bad Idea?   203
Chapter 38
   Gettin' Out of Dodge: The "Boom-Boom" Strategy   207
Chapter 39
   The Professional Gambler's Paradox   211
Chapter 40
   The 10 Basic Rules of Gambling   215
Chapter 41
   The Top 10 Gambling Mistakes   217
Chapter 42
   Rounding 3rd and Heading Home,   221
   Wrapping Up This Little Tome

Appendix A
   Andy Glazer's *Simplified* Blackjack Strategy   225

Appendix B
   Blackjack Basic Strategy Table   229

Appendix C
   Glossary   231

Index   249

Introduction

Roughly 30 million Americans will take about 150 million trips to casinos this year. Professional gamblers will set forth on a tiny, tiny fraction of those trips. All the rest will be taken by people who, while wanting to win, are mostly interested in having fun.

Although there are many gambling books available to guide such journeys, very few of them serve this vast group of recreational gamblers well. Most of the really good books are written by professionals for other professionals, or for those with professional aspirations. The lessons they offer, while often brilliant, are usually too math-heavy, intense, or demanding in hours of study to be of any significant practical use to a recreational player.

Bookstores also carry quite a few simple or introductory books about gambling, but most of these miss the mark too far in the other direction, either explaining only the most basic rules of the games, or offering words of encouragement that can't possibly be justified by an author with a conscience. Take "Become a big winner at craps!," for example. It isn't possible to become a big winner at craps. It's certainly possible to have big winning sessions, or days, or even years, but eventually the house odds will catch up with you, and anyone who tries to promote his or her writing with such false claims falls a little short ethically.

I think it's interesting to note that if I'd had my way, this book would have been titled "Casino Self-Defense," and the subtitle would have been "Wisdom, Humor, and Easy-to-Remember Tips for Your Gambling Vacations." The title I wound up negotiating with my otherwise marvelous publisher was something of a compromise. Career

Press quite understandably wanted a title that emphasized winning (originally suggesting "The Winner's Guide to Casino Gambling," which, fortunately, was already taken), and I had my funky principles about not unduly encouraging people, and a negotiation of 20 phone calls, e-mails, and faxes got us to the title you see. I stood my ground as strongly as I could because I believe the attitude you bring to your gambling will have a dramatic impact on both your financial and emotional results. At the same time I have to admit that Career Press had a point with its view that my message wouldn't do much good if no one bought the book.

So, now firmly convinced that the editors at Career Press and I could hammer out the difficulties in the Middle East in about a week, what I have created is a book that can and does live up to a few promises:

First, it is *easy to read and digest.* I wrote *Casino Gambling the Smart Way* so that both experienced and novice players could read it casually, in small bites, without needing to study a complicated system or practice for hours and hours. Although math is near and dear to me, I have left the heavy math out entirely and refer even to simple math as little as possible: You don't need it to apply the lessons.

I've made the book funny because most people gamble to have fun, and learning more about it doesn't have to be agonizing or boring. I also think that the humor and anecdotes will make the lessons easier to remember. That's why I've written the book conversationally, rather than in some erudite, intimidating style. I intentionally violate a grammatical rule here and there, to boldly go into what will feel more like a conversation than a lecture.

Second, the book is *honest.* By that I mean I am committed to not raising your expectations to an unrealistic level just to sell books. I'll never promote this book by saying, "Read *Casino Gambling the Smart Way* and become a winner!" This book's subtitle indicates that by playing smart you can win *more* money than you have been winning, but *not* that you will become a winner. What I can say, with a completely clear conscience and indeed a very firm conviction of truth, is, "Read this book and your results will improve dramatically!" You will win more often and, when you do lose, you will lose less.

Unless you leave the ranks of the recreational gambler to become a professional (and I discuss some reasons why you shouldn't in Chapter 39, "The Professional Gambler's Paradox"), you won't become a long-term *financial* winner, because at most games there is no getting completely around the house percentages, although you can certainly reduce them dramatically. Your results will *feel* like long-term success, though, because your results will improve and you'll have more fun. Your gambling will become a cost-effective hobby, much as scuba-diving, attending professional sporting events, travel, or clothes-shopping can be cost-effective hobbies. Read *Casino Gambling the Smart Way*, and the amount you spend on gambling will start to bear a more rational relationship to the amount of fun you have gambling.

Third, the book *acknowledges that you are an individual*, with your own unique desires, feelings, goals, and talents. As much as possible I have tried to avoid dictating that you "must" do this or that. In the main, I try to explain choices, possibilities, and options, and then let you make your own decisions.

As you'll discover on your ride through *Casino Gambling the Smart Way*, I've been gambling in casinos for almost 30 years. In the 1970s, I paid a good deal of my college and law school tuition with money I won playing blackjack in Las Vegas. In the mid-1980s, I earned my living playing backgammon, winning some big national and international tournaments. And for two years in the mid-1990s, I earned my living playing poker.

These bursts of gambling as a professional have been sandwiched between longer stretches in "respectable" jobs (many of which involved either writing, or teaching at various colleges, universities, and private educational centers), but even while working in the mainstream, I've gambled for fun and profit as a hobby.

As a result of this combination of teaching, writing, and gaming expertise, I think you're in pretty good hands here, but you'll be able to judge for yourself soon enough.

Like driving a car, crossing the street, or eating in new restaurants, gambling has its risks, and it gets a bad name because of the sadly large number of people who cannot control their gambling addictions. Because it's hard to predict just who the next gambling addict will be, I'm not anxious to encourage people to gamble, if they don't do so already.

The vast majority of people who gamble, though, are not addicts or problem gamblers. Like me, they like taking a little risk, like playing daredevil with their own personal fear/greed index, and they find the adult fantasy world of Las Vegas and other gambling towns a welcome break from everyday life.

For that vast majority, I offer *Casino Gambling the Smart Way* as a fun tool to make your hobby more affordable and in turn enjoyable. If you like it, you might want to attend one of my seminars; I travel around the country teaching for my company, Casino Conquests. You can also visit our Web site at www.casinoconquests.com. I make the same promises in all forms of my educational endeavors: The material will be easy to digest, entertaining, honest, and it will treat you with respect.

If you're fairly new to gambling, make sure you make good use of the Glossary. It's more detailed than most glossaries, and you'll find some funny stories there, too.

Douglas Adams fans may notice that this book has 42 chapters. That's a coincidence, just like everything else you ever thought was a coincidence, was a coincidence.

If you find that the material in *Casino Gambling the Smart Way* helps you, I'd love to hear from you (you can write to me through the publisher; send e-mail through our Web site; or call 1-888-ODDS-WIN). One of the reasons I no longer make my living gambling is that I wanted to move away from an "I Win, You Lose" lifestyle. At Casino Conquests, I win, and so do you, and I never tire of hearing that we're both richer for having crossed paths.

—Andy Glazer

Preface

Sed quis custodiet ipsos custudios?
(But who is to guard the guards themselves?)

My desire to please my high school Latin teacher, Mr. Thomas Young, aside, the title of this Preface offers a nearly 2,000-year-old important question to anyone preparing to learn something about gambling—once you've recognized that your gambling teachers are in effect guards of your money.

In three words: *Consider the source.*

Casinos frequently offer gaming instruction to novices. Sometimes these are live lessons in the casino itself, and sometimes they take the form of in-room, closed-circuit TV. In the near future (probably by the time you're reading this), instruction will be available on free-standing kiosks within casinos. Consider the following paragraph, excerpted from a press release about these new kiosks:

> (Company name omitted) provides in-room gaming programming for hotel casinos. Its programming is produced in their studios in Las Vegas, and distributed to client hotel casinos on a closed-circuit basis with a state-of-the-art technology developed by (omitted). The programming is designed to entertain and educate guests while acting as a marketing tool for the casinos and advertisers.

Okay, so there is a little education going on...amidst the entertainment, which is fine, and amidst the marketing, which isn't so fine.

Casino-sponsored instruction in how to gamble is designed with one purpose in mind: to extract, either in the short run or the long run, the maximum dollars from casino customers. There will be some very accurate and useful information provided, because the novice will lose too quickly if he or she doesn't possess some knowledge. But there will also be *less* useful information provided, some of it perhaps very subtle, and there's no way for the novice to be able to separate the good from the bad.

So when a casino, a casino shill, a casino-sponsored company, or indeed anyone whose livelihood depends on a good relationship with casinos tries to teach you how to gamble, consider the source, and consider just how good a job this particular "guard" of your money is motivated to do.

Similarly, when you're examining other gambling books, writings, or seminars, be cautious about those that are enthusiastically endorsed by casino executives. Really now, why would a casino executive want to support a book which *truly* helps players lose less? I don't take money from casinos, I don't use casino mailing lists to market my books or seminars, and I don't do anything that makes me or Casino Conquests reliant on casino goodwill, because I don't want my educational integrity compromised. If a casino executive publicly endorses *this* book, it's probably because he or she read this Preface!

PART ONE:

BEFORE YOU LEAVE FOR LAS VEGAS...

Chapter 1

♣

Float Like a Butterfly, Sting Like a Bee: Play With the Style of Muhammed Ali

During his prime, Muhammed Ali provided one of the great shows in boxing history. With his famous "float like a butterfly, sting like a bee" style, Ali used superior speed and tactics to hit stronger opponents like Sonny Liston and Joe Frazier, and then moved away before they could hit him back.

Sadly, later in his career he switched to another now-famous style that he called "rope-a-dope." This entailed leaning back onto the ropes, letting his opponents hit him repeatedly, and then attacking when they tired. It worked—just ask the then-young and seemingly invincible George Foreman—but in the long run it took quite a toll on Ali's mind and body.

Why this trip down boxing's memory lane? I'm not waxing nostalgic, and I'm not writing about betting on boxing. Instead, I'm going to show you some important parallels between your trip to the casino, and a heavyweight boxing match.

In this corner, the Champion, weighing in at about 20 billion pounds, 200' tall, with a record of 847,932 wins and 2,356 losses, the Casino (boooo!).

And in this corner, the Challenger, weighing in at 150 lbs., 5'9", with a record of 3 wins, 6 losses and 8 "I pretty much broke evens," the Reader (yeah!).

Okay, on whom do you want to bet?

The casino has just about everything going for it: experience, bankroll, and, most importantly, the odds. Over the long run, the odds win. As fights go, this looks like a mismatch: You don't have the experience, you don't have the bankroll, and you don't have the odds going for you (unless you're a blackjack card counter, a video poker expert, or you're taking advantage of a short-term casino promotion).

Given that reality, how would you like to approach your upcoming fight with the casino? Do you want to stand toe-to-toe, trading heavy punch for heavy punch? Do you want to lean back on the ropes, absorbing every bit of punishment that the casino can dish out and, then, when the casino tires, *Bam!*, knock it out?

Or would you rather bob and weave, keep moving, not let the casino get a clean shot at you, sting 'em quick and then move away, scoring enough points to win a decision? That's floating like a butterfly, stinging like a bee...and it can work for you. You better hope that it can because, unlike George Foreman, casinos don't get tired.

The player employing the gaming equivalent of rope-a-dope spends every possible hour at the tables or slots during a Vegas trip, often skipping meals and sleep. Win some, lose some, it doesn't matter, just keep at it because, after all, the reason you came was to play, right? They don't have gambling back home.

People who employ the rope-a-dope strategy are not only asking for trouble, they're refusing to bask in whatever glory and winning feelings Fate offers in the course of a trip. To the rope-a-doper, a winning streak offers another great reason to keep playing.

The "float like a butterfly, sting like a bee" player treats a win streak differently. After winning a significant sum, a "stinger" takes a break. It could be to walk around town a little, have lunch, go to a show, play tennis, or just watch others gambling. No matter what the diversion, the stinger has a bit of a spring in his or her step, is walking proud, feeling like a winner, getting to enjoy the taste of victory.

The psychology is a bit different during a losing streak. Frazier just hit you upside the head and you're a bit dizzy. Instead of moving in to get whacked while you can't defend yourself, you keep moving and use those great legs to stay away from him. You still take a break, except instead of doing it to bask in victory, you're doing it to survive. Think it sounds like you're playing games with yourself? Right on. You came to town to play games and this one doesn't involve a house percentage.

Are my reasons for "floating" purely psychological? Not at all. Because casino games create a long-term mathematical advantage for the house, you enjoy best results by giving the house as few shots at you as possible, and by not letting house percentages wear down your bankroll. Pauses in the action help keep your bankroll intact.

I'm *not* saying quit as soon as you win a bet or two—that would be silly. Instead, be willing to breathe in the taste of victory. You go to Las Vegas and other gambling destinations because you view gambling as fun. What I propose is to expand your definition of fun to include not merely playing, but also walking around feeling like a winner.

Eventually you'll go back to the tables, and maybe you'll win some more, or maybe you'll lose. Even if you do lose, though, they can't take away those fun hours you had feeling like a winner!

Perhaps the ultimate in "floating like a butterfly" is what I call a "Long March." Start at any point on the strip, enter a casino, and play until you've won or lost a set amount, say $50. As soon as that happens, cash in and walk to the next casino, where, once again, you play until you hit plus or minus $50.

What with all the walking and cashing in, a Long March gives you a chance to see a lot of different casinos while never getting blasted anywhere. You can create all sorts of variations, like "The Optimist March" (staying until either you win $100 or lose $50). Plug in whatever numbers you want.

Each time you sting 'em and move on, that walk to the next casino is a bouncy one. And when they sting you instead, you get to pat yourself on the back for getting the heck out of there before they hurt you worse.

Fighting a heavyweight is tough enough without just standing there and getting clubbed. If you value your bankroll, float a little here and sting a little there. Not only will you win more rounds, you'll have a better chance in the overall fight. "Ladies and gentlemen, we have a split decision...."

Chapter 2

◆

Who Ya Tryin' to Impress?

Bad Brian walked up to the roulette table, neatly placed down a stack of black $100 chips, and announced, "$2,000 on red." The croupier eyed the chips and alerted his supervisor to the large bet by calling over his shoulder, "Black checks play."

"Ooooh, you're cute," said the flashy blonde who'd been sitting alone at the table. Just the reaction Bad Brian had been hoping for.

"No more bets," called the croupier. "No more bets."

"You *are* pretty cute," the blonde repeated. "Do you play here much?"

"Twenty four, *black*," called the croupier, sweeping in Bad Brian's chips.

"Wow, that's the last of it," gulped Bad Brian. "Want to go get a drink?"

"You were cuter a little while ago," said the blonde, picking up her chips and walking away.

Pardon the sexist and stereotypical tale, but it makes a point. For some reason, a lot of people pick Las Vegas as the place they want to impress others. Maybe it's because

Vegas is a fantasy world to begin with, maybe it's because so many movies have been made with high roller scenes that the image has become some people's reality.

Whatever your motivation might be, trying to impress someone else with big bets is usually a bad idea. We've already seen reason number one: Even if you succeed, usually those you're trying to impress *remain* impressed only while you're winning. Vegas loves a winner, and if it doesn't hate a loser, it sure doesn't get excited by one.

So let's take a look at just whom you might be trying to impress with your big play, and how likely you are to achieve your goal.

1. The dealer. Sounds crazy, I know, but I've seen it happen often. A rated player arrives at the craps table and a dealer announces to the table, "Okay, now we're going to see some action!" The player immediately makes a big show of spreading lots of bets around the table and flinging a lot of insider lingo about ("A hundred on the line, gimme the six and eight, gimme a hundred comin' every time, all the hard ways for a nickel, action always working, and bet a horn for the boys." Wow, you can Crapspeak! You're really cool. May I touch the hem of your robe, sire?), to live up to reputation the dealer has announced. In this example there is obviously an element of trying to impress the other players, too.

The problem with trying to impress the dealer is that you're almost certainly doing the exact opposite. If you bet big responding to dealer encouragement, the dealer looks at you like a lab rat who can easily be talked into pressing the food pellet button. If the dealer hasn't said anything, he or she still probably thinks you're foolish for betting so heavily. Finally, no matter how big your betting action is, unless it's the dealer's first day on the job, he or she has seen *lots* bigger action.

And why should you care if you impress the dealer, anyway?

2. Unknown fellow players. This sort of play usually involves trying to impress the opposite sex and, like Bad Brian's experience, it usually only works if you win.

I suspect that most members of the opposite sex whom you'd want to know for more than a quick visit to your hotel room would be more impressed by reasonable play and friendly conversation than by big bets. And although there are certainly people of both sexes who hang around casinos looking to meet high rollers, you don't have to bet big to exchange money for sex. You can skip the betting and move directly on to the exchange, if that's what you're looking for.

I have a friend who met his wife playing blackjack in the Bahamas. Each of them was playing the table minimum. The smile and the friendly conversation was what mattered.

3. Known fellow players. So you went gambling with a buddy, or maybe a girlfriend/boyfriend. What does big betting do?

If you really *are* good friends, big betting doesn't change a thing, except maybe your friend is concerned for your bankroll. If you aren't good friends, do you think gambling big will win someone over? Is that the kind of friend you want?

And if you're on a weekend fling, I have big news for you: The time when you needed to impress your playmate was when you asked him/her to go along. He or she *already* said yes. This one's already in the bag, unless you go broke and start acting like a jerk. So you don't have much to gain, and maybe lots to lose.

4. Yourself. Huh? Why or how would you bet to impress yourself? Actually, this one makes more sense to me than any of the others...still not *good* sense, but better than the other three.

It's easy to see how someone who doubts his or her own courage could decide to bet big, just as that same person might decide to go bungee-jumping or parachute jumping: a self-imposed test of nerve.

I really can't argue with this. You're the only one who knows how badly you feel about your own perceived lack of nerve, and if you feel you must do something to prove yourself, taking risks with your money seems a lot smarter than taking risks with your life.

On the other hand, I wonder how effective taking this sort of risk will really be. Suppose you do bet big, and get away with it. What happens the next time you're in Las Vegas? If you go back to betting sensibly, will you get down on yourself for losing your nerve? If that's the case, if you have to keep betting big to keep from despising yourself, maybe you should invest some of the money you were thinking about betting in some kind of counseling or therapy. The results will probably be more effective, longer-lasting, and get to the root of the problem, instead of treating the symptoms.

Well, that's pretty much everyone I can think of whom you might be trying to impress, and we didn't find too many good reasons. If you want to bet big just because you like the thrills, and you can afford to lose, go right ahead.

If, on the other hand, you want to bet big because you want to impress someone else, you probably *will* create an impression—all bad. And if somehow you do manage to look cute to the flashy blonde, it probably won't be for very long.

Chapter 3

♥

Gaming Vacations Are Not All Created Equal

What's the difference between a vacation trip to a casino destination like Las Vegas, and one like Lake Tahoe or the Bahamas?

If you answered, "It's easier to move from casino to casino in Las Vegas," give yourself a (-10) score. You've missed the point of the question.

Gambling can fit into a vacation in one of two ways: Either it's the primary attraction (and even with all of the family entertainment now installed in Las Vegas, gambling is certainly the primary attraction there), or it's a secondary diversion.

When you go to Lake Tahoe, you're probably going for the gorgeous scenery, or to do some skiing, and you figure some casino gambling will make for a pleasant après ski. When you go to the Bahamas, it's fun in the sun time, with some jet skiing, parasailing, or snorkeling thrown in... and the casino stands ready as an evening diversion when the sun is done.

Unless you picked Tahoe or the Bahamas as a compromise vacation—your spouse wanting to relax and you wanting to stack the chips—you can risk blowing what would otherwise be a great trip by indulging in heavy casino action. Playing a little is okay, but stepping up to the plate with $25 or $100 chips, or hitting the $5 slots, is asking for trouble.

Suppose these destinations didn't have any gambling. You could still have a great time there, and indeed you probably do have a great time while outside the casino. Now suppose that your skiing or fun in the sun gets overshadowed by a big loss at the casino. How are you going to feel the next day?

If you lose your shirt the first night in the Bahamas, not only are you going to get a bad sunburn the next day, but you're likely to suffer from a bad attitude, too. Those steel bands which seemed so charming the first day become "those $%!&*$#! steel bands," $45 for a scooter rental now seems like a lot of money, and the lobster dinner at the fancy place seems like a rip-off.

In short, you've cast a black cloud over what should have been a great time. And if you have a great trip for four days and then blow a wad in the casino the final night, the only afterglow left from your vacation is the sunburn, and that's going to start peeling soon enough.

"Wait a minute," you say. "Why are you assuming I'm going to lose? What if I win a bundle? Then my fun vacation is even more fun!"

Maybe. Let's be charitable and say that you stand a 50-50 chance of coming out a winner (and no matter what you tell your friends, deep down you know the real odds are worse than that). Let's further say that you're going to take four such trips in the course of two years.

I maintain that four "definitely fun" (no or slight gambling) vacations provide much more fun and relaxation than two "great" (win at gambling) vacations and two "ruined" (lost a bundle gambling) vacations.

Now, I'm not down on a little gambling at a glamorous resort. Most people aren't going to get upset by losing $50, or $100, or $200. If you can set a reasonable loss limit and stick to it even after sampling rum punches throughout the afternoon, go have fun. But when you drop a big number, life tastes different for a little while.

Of course, if losing a bundle really won't ruin your vacation, then by all means plunge on in. Most people, though, are betting more than they think when they start gambling heavily on a "fun" vacation. They're betting their money—and their vacation, too.

When your destination is *primarily* a gambling destination, be it Las Vegas or an Indian casino, that's a different story. You're not risking anything beyond your bets, because you knew going in that gambling was going to be the trip's focus. Win and have a fun trip, lose and have a not-so-fun trip. There's no extra risk.

But when you're already a "vacation winner" *before* you start playing, I'd suggest you think twice before you ante up heavily. There's probably more at stake than you realize.

Chapter 4

♠

If You
Bring $300 to Lose,
You Will!

I can't even begin to guess how many people I've met who tell me that they play sensibly because they "bring $300 to lose," or "bring $50 to lose," or some other such number, when they go to Las Vegas.

That's what I call a good news/bad news kind of attitude. The good news, the part I really love, is the stated intent to hold losses to a set limit. That kind of discipline is critical if you're going to gamble as a hobby. Without it, one nightmarish trip can break you: I've seen it happen often enough (never yet, knock wood, to me).

By setting a loss limit, you protect yourself from all kinds of trouble. If you lose your $300 limit the first day of a three-day trip, you might feel dumb on days two and three, but there are all sorts of roller coasters, lounge acts, golf courses, and other forms of entertainment in Las Vegas that aren't so bad. And two days of feeling dumb feels a heck of a lot better than 365 days of feeling broke.

The bad news is that the choice of words, "I brought $300 to lose," makes it a near certainty that the speaker will accomplish this "goal"—that is, lose the $300.

It might seem like I'm mincing words (after all, I'm a recovered lawyer): What the heck's the difference between saying, "I brought $300 to lose," and, "I set a loss limit of $300"? I don't think I am mincing words. I think the difference is maybe half of that $300.

Huh? Or, as my friends south of the border would say, "Que?"

Here's the reason. When you say, "I brought $300 to lose," you are expecting, both consciously and subconsciously, to lose. You know you're going for a good time, for some entertainment, and you figure $300 is the amount Las Vegas will charge you for the entertainment.

More to the point, because you know you're going to lose the $300, *it doesn't matter very much what games you play, or how well you play them, because you're "going to lose" the $300 anyway!*

In some ways, that's empowering, or at least pain-reducing. Lose a $10 bet? So what? You're going to lose $300 anyway. The $10 loss is simply part of an inevitable process. And because it doesn't matter what games you play or how well you play them, you'll probably play games that can knock you out quickly, or play games like blackjack without the kind of skill that can give you a fighting chance.

On the other hand, if your attitude is, "I'm setting a loss limit of $300," you're not planning on losing $300, you're just refusing to lose any more than your limit—a very different approach.

With the loss limit approach, you haven't accepted defeat. You want to win, you're going to do your best to win, but if things go badly, you're going to get stung only for $300.

When the "brought $300 to lose" person steps up to a craps table, he or she bets more or less randomly. A Field bet here, a Hardway bet there, an "Any Craps" bet (because the last person to bet it won), and even, I shudder to think of it, a Big Six/Big Eight bet (so conveniently located at the edge of the table). This bettor scatters money about the craps table like Johnny Appleseed scattering seeds before the wind—but unlike Johnny, won't reap much.

When a Loss Limiter steps up to a craps table, he or she has probably taken the time to learn that Hardway bets lose much faster than Pass Line bets, and so stays away from them. The Loss Limiter doesn't look out over a sea of slot machines and think all slots are created equal. He or she knows that some machines pay more regularly than others, or that some progressive payoffs are much better deals than others.

In short, the Loss Limiter comes to Las Vegas ready for a battle. True, the odds favor the casino, but by understanding that there is a chance to win if one plays well, the Loss Limiter earns an occasional winning trip, and doesn't always lose the limit.

The "brought $300 to lose" person is probably a very casual, very occasional gambler, and there's nothing wrong with that. There's no law that says everyone who gambles has to wring the best possible deal out of the casino, or play like an expert. There are elements of work and effort involved in that approach that don't fit everyone's notion of a fun vacation.

But if you're going to Las Vegas with the notion of coming home a winner once in a while, don't bring $300 to lose. Bring your best effort, set and stick to a loss limit, and you won't be spending day three working on your suntan.

Chapter 5

♣

Play It Cool
When You Arrive,
and Your Bankroll
Will Survive

Beating the odds on a Las Vegas trip is tough enough without trying to do it under less than ideal circumstances. Most people can see that playing when drunk, tired, angry, upset, or desperate all qualify as "less than ideal circumstances," and so I won't preach to the choir.

But almost everyone plays under one particular handicap without recognizing it as such. They play in the first few hours after their arrival, and that's a dangerous time.

If you're playing at a local casino, or you're taking a one-day trip, you don't have much of a choice. Either you play soon after you arrive, or the trip doesn't make sense. You came to gamble, and the trip probably wasn't long or tiring, so go ahead and play. At least if you lose your stake in a hurry, you aren't stuck in town for three days with nothing to do.

If your trip involves more of a journey, though, and if you plan on staying for a few days, you most definitely have a choice of when to dive in. I suggest fairly strongly that you consider relaxing a little before you take the big plunge.

Why? Think about your mental, physical, emotional, and financial states when you first arrive. If you flew or drove any kind of distance, you're probably a little tired or jet-lagged. You're probably a little excited at the thought of getting to the tables or slots, and your heart is racing a bit. Your pockets are full of cash and your heart full of optimism.

You are, in other words, a chicken perfectly ready to be plucked. Caution? Are you kidding, I just got here! Discipline? Come on, do you think I sat on that plane for four hours so I could be disciplined?

Indeed, given the mood in which most people arrive in Vegas, they might as well get started by having Michael Buffer (the tuxedoed boxing announcer who's noted for his dramatic "let's get ready to rumble" introduction) boom into his microphone, "Let's get ready to G-A-M-B-L-E...."

Easy does it! You're going to be here for a few days. The tables and slots are open 24 hours a day. There are going to be *plenty* of opportunities to gamble. You might ask what the difference is: Gamble now, gamble later, it's still gambling.

The difference is that you are not quite yourself when you first arrive. Adrenaline is up, reasoning is down. A three-day trip is a marathon, not a sprint, and calls for different tactics. Bolting into action before you're rested and prepared isn't optimal strategy.

Let's look at it a different way. Suppose you were taking a four-hour plane flight to New York for a big job interview. Would you make your reservations for a flight that landed two hours before the interview? Almost certainly not, because you know you'd be tired, and you'd want a good night's sleep and a chance to settle down from the trip before asking yourself to perform at the very peak of your abilities.

Do you really want to take the casino on at less than your best? I thought we'd already covered that when I mentioned playing drunk, tired, angry, upset, or desperate.

There are other good reasons to show a little restraint. Let's say you dive right in, and you either lose a lot or win a lot the very first night. How does the rest of the trip play out?

If you win a lot the first night, you certainly have a fun first night. But where do you go from there? If you're a smart, disciplined player, you might say, "Okay, I'm up $1,000, I'm going to take at least $400 of it home with me."

That's an admirable way to plan, yet it locks you into a budget of $600 for the rest of the trip if things start going badly. True, you get the pleasure of going home a winner, but you probably don't get the action you wanted during the trip.

Of course, maybe your hot streak doesn't end that first night. Maybe you'll just keep right on winning without ever slowing down. That's great if it happens, and if it does, your first night plunge works out just fine. But this doesn't actually happen very often, and you know it.

Let's look at the more likely scenario, that by diving in big right away, you lose big. Now your first night's sleep isn't so great, you've lost all or part of your stake, you're chiding yourself for losing so fast, and you are faced with a choice between throttling down your play for the rest of the trip or increasing the amount you were willing to lose over the course of the trip. Neither of those choices seems appealing.

Now let's envision a relaxed first night. You check into your hotel, get a decent meal, and take the time to plan what if any non-gaming activities you're going to enjoy while in town. You make your show reservations now, if you haven't already (I suggest paying in full in advance, because if the gambling goes poorly you might not want to fork it over later). You walk around town and check out what new casinos or attractions might have opened.

You can probably go ahead and play a little, because that is, after all, what you came to do. But play for low stakes, for a reasonable period of time, and make sure you get a good night's rest. You go to sleep quite proud of your maturity and self-control, and wake up ready to take on the world.

Sounds like a better second day, doesn't it?

Some people will claim that by taking it easy the first night, you're simply postponing whatever will happen later. I disagree, both because you're not in peak form the first night, and because waking up the next morning feeling proud of your self-discipline sets a positive tone for the rest of the trip.

If you're a slot player, this warning isn't quite as important, because slot play doesn't lend itself to sudden plunges, foolish bets, or mistakes in play, but I still like the idea of reminding yourself that you can stop or start any time you want.

I believe that if you lie low the first night, and take on the town only when you're refreshed and confident, you will vastly improve your chances not only of avoiding an early blowout, but also for an overall winning trip. If the idea of this small measure of self-discipline seems impossible to you, you should leave your credit cards at home, because when you ask for trouble, Las Vegas is usually willing to provide it.

Part Two:

Gambling Systems and Other Bad Ideas

Chapter 6

♦

The Not-So-Great Martingale Debate

"Pssst!" said the guy in the alley. "Ya wanna buy a system?"

A system! Every player's dream! It seemed almost too good to be true, though, so I figured I better check it out.

"How do I know it's any good?" I asked.

"I've won lots with it," said the guy, and indeed the fine cut of his faded polyester jacket seemed to hint of Monte Carlo days-gone-by. "It's only 50 bucks, and if ya don't win, come back tomorrow and I'll give ya yer money back."

A 100-percent money-back guarantee! How could I do better than that? But I was still cautious. "Tell me the system first—then the $50."

"Hey, kid, you're pretty sharp—been around the block a few times, I'll bet. Some guys would just fork over the $50 without thinkin' that I might run off before I gave 'em the valuable information."

"I was born in the morning, but it wasn't *yesterday* morning," I said, pretty wittily, I thought.

"Okay here's the deal. Ya go into the casino and ya make a minimum bet at yer favorite game. What's yer favorite game?"

"Blackjack. I'm working on becoming a card counter."

"Hey, that's great kid, I used to do that before I got barred by all the big casinos, that's why I gotta make a living selling my system now. Anyway, ya go make a $5 bet. If ya win, ya make another $5 bet. Ya keep bettin' the minimum until ya lose a bet."

"What happens then?"

"This here's the secret. Ya double up and make a $10 bet! If ya win, ya lost $5 on the hand before, but ya win $10 here, so you're up a fiver, and ya go back to $5 bets. And if ya lose the ten-spot, ya double up again, to $20."

"So...if I win when I bet the $20, I lost my $5 and $10 bets—a total of $15—but then I win $20, so I still win five bucks overall, right?"

The guy looked impressed. "Pretty sharp, kid. So what happens if ya keep losin'?"

"Well, I guess I would bet $40—I'd have lost $5, $10 and $20, that's $35—so I'd still win five bucks. And if I lose the $40, I'd bet $80...yeah, *every time* I wind up winning five bucks. What a great system! Here's your $50, and it's cheap at the price!"

And so I (not really...thankfully this story is the one piece of fiction in the whole book) headed off into the sunset, ready to make a killing, $5 at a time. In reality, the casino would be doing all the killing, because the guy in the alley was selling what's called a "Martingale" system, one of the oldest and worst betting systems known to man or woman, and curiously one that many players seem to invent themselves.

A Martingale "double-up after losing" system (there are variations such as "double-up and add a dollar," but they're all the same for purposes of this discussion) inevitably fails for two reasons:

First, each and every bet you make is a separate and distinct entity from your other bets, and each such separate entity is a slight underdog. There is no way to combine several disadvantage bets into one advantage bet. When you were young, this rule was known as "two wrongs don't make a right."

Second, all Martingalers suffer from a lack of either forethought or experience, because *the system breaks down after a relatively short losing streak*. Let's say we use the $5 double-up method proposed by our polyester-clad friend, The Guy in the Alley. How quickly do we reach the table limit?

Hand 1—$5	Hand 5—$80
Hand 2—$10	Hand 6—$160
Hand 3—$20	Hand 7—$320
Hand 4—$40	Hand 8—$640

Uh, oh. If you're at a table with a $500 limit (the most common kind with $5 minimums), you can't make Hand 8. True, you can find $5 tables with a higher limit (as much as $10,000), but these are less common, and merely postpone the problem by a few bets.

So the big problem arrives when you hit a long losing streak. A seven-hand streak rates to happen once every few hours (the longer streaks, which would break you at higher limit tables, happen less frequently; I'm going to discuss the more common $500 limit here). You can't make the eighth bet; you can only bet $500, which does *not* win your $5; you're $140 short, *if* you win the $500 bet, a big *if*.

There is a psychological component at work, too. Arriving at the eighth bet, you are already a $635 loser (5+10+20+40+80+160+320). Unless you've already had a *lot* of $5 victories, you're a loser *before* you try to make that next bet. So will you now have the courage (if that's the right word) or bankroll to plunk down $500? What if that loses?

If it does lose, you're down $1,135 (the $635 plus the $500), with no rule that says you're going to win the next hand, or the hand after that. You're now outside your system: You're just someone making $500 bets. Correct me if I'm wrong, but doesn't betting $500 to try to win $5 seem...nuts? Finding a table with a higher limit only postpones the problem. Would you, as a $5 player, pull $5,120 out of your wallet to make Hand 11, especially knowing that if you lost, you couldn't make a $10,240 bet? Didn't think so.

In practice, most Martingale players ditch the system before they hit the maximum bet. The first time they have to spring for $160, or maybe $320, they lose their nerve, which thankfully saves a few dollars, though not as many as they could have saved by avoiding the Martingale mess in the first place.

So there lies the Martingale system, may it rest in peace. You can play it for 10 or 20 minutes and get lucky— but you can get lucky just as easily *without* a system that inevitably leads to ruin. You could also start your seven-hand losing streak on Hand 1, and then there's only one way to get even. Of course, if you don't already own a faded polyester jacket, you might need a little cash for startup expenses....

Chapter 7

♥

One-Hour
(and Three-Year)
Martinizing

I was a long-haired, know-it-all college kid when I first met my step-uncle, Martin, in the store his father had started.

"So you're Andrew, huh?" he said, offering a handshake. "I've been looking forward to meeting you. I hear you're pretty good at blackjack."

"I play a little," I said.

"Well, I play craps," said Martin. "I've been to Atlantic City 20 times and I haven't lost yet. I've made $50,000 with my system."

(Now, Andrew, this is a new family member, it isn't polite to snort or laugh out loud.)

"Really?" I said, sounding as impressed as my limited theatrical background would allow. "You've never lost?"

"Nope, not even once. My system is unbeatable."

"Wow," I said, mentally calculating the odds that a furniture salesman from New Jersey would be the first man in the history of the human race to figure out a way to beat the craps tables long-term. The results weren't promising, but I couldn't resist hearing him out.

(Note to the reader: I'm relaying here, word-for-word, our actual conversation. It contained a lot of what I call "Crapspeak," and if you're new to craps, you might want to keep the Glossary handy...and if it still seems confusing, just translate it all as "Martin was playing with a simple pattern that he considered a system," and stay with me, because the lesson is important, whether you understand craps or not.)

"So, would you mind telling me what your system is? I mean, unless it's a secret."

"No, I'll tell you," he said, "After all you're in my family now." (You can choose your friends, but you can't choose...). He continued, "First, I bet the Pass Line."

"Got it," I said, mentally noting the house's 1.41-percent advantage.

"Then I take full single odds (better; that's a fair, even-money bet, but of course still no favorite), and I make a Come bet every time and take full odds on the Come bets."

A Come bet offers exactly the same odds as a Pass Line bet; it's just a way of keeping the action going faster. So far, nothing very radical. "And then what?" I asked, waiting for the big secret.

"That's it," he said. "It always wins. Whenever I crap out, I get paid for the seven by winning the Come bet, so that cuts some of my losses, and until I throw the seven, I'm collecting on all the numbers."

"That's it?" I exclaimed, my limited theatrical background failing me. "You've won 20 trips in a row with that system?"

"Yup. $50,000."

"Congratulations," I said in my best know-it-all (yet envious) college-kid tone. "You've been very lucky. You're playing craps reasonably intelligently, given that you're playing craps at all, but you've just been lucky. That's not a system. Or at least it's not a system that rates to continue winning."

"Well, youngster," he said, a little testily (I knew he was going to play that card sooner or later. He probably would have tried "shorty" but I'm 6'3"), "I've made my money and I have my results. You've got your game and I've got mine. It's money in the bank."

"Okay, well, maybe you're right," I said, not wanting to create a problem with Thanksgiving seating for the next 20 years. "This is some nice furniture you have in here."

It *was* nice furniture, a good thing, because good old Uncle Martin's unshakable belief in his system cost him, over the next three years, not merely the $50,000 that he had already allegedly won, but another gigantic, colossal chunk of change on top of it (in the name of avoiding an even bigger family ruckus than this chapter will already no doubt cause, I will refrain from stating just *how* gigantic or colossal).

How could he lose so much? Because Martin had been lucky at the start of his gaming "career," he became convinced that his system had meaning. Because he had faith in the system, he kept playing long after someone else would have given up. I took to calling system play "Martinizing," after my step-uncle and his three-year trip to the cleaners.

Does this tale mean that it's always bad to play a system? Not at all. Playing a system just means you're employing some kind of pattern, rather than betting or playing randomly, and that sounds promising enough.

The danger to system play isn't the system, it's the *belief* in the system, the belief that somehow a pattern of betting or playing will change the fundamental nature of the game you're playing. It won't...but it can accomplish something less, such as making a game more fun.

For example, I have a craps system that I use in those rare times when I play craps for pleasure. I look carefully at the shooter, and use my psychic powers to determine if the shooter is a Winner or a Loser. Usually I decide Loser and bet Don't Pass. If I get a Winner vibe, I bet the Pass Line.

Do I believe in my system? Of course not. I do believe that intuition has a place in certain types of gambling, but once I've gone as far as logic or math can take me (see Chapter 23 for more about this), I certainly don't have psychic powers usable in the gaming arena, and my system hasn't changed my long-term expected results. It's just the pattern I employ when playing, a game within the game. Mathematically it means nothing, just like roulette systems that tell you to bet red after black has come up three times in a row (or the equally silly systems that tell you to bet red after *red* has come up three times in a row).

The big difference is that the system player who believes in a system will make unreasonably large bets, or make bets that he or she cannot afford to lose, because of the belief. When that happens, a system is no longer just a pattern, it's bad money management—and that will lead to ruin faster than you can say, "You ween again, monsieur, you have broken zee bank."

Of course, it is possible to finish with a small fortune while betting a system...as long as you started out with a large fortune! So the next time some well-meaning soul sings the praises of his or her gaming system, thank 'em with your best theatrical effort, compliment 'em on their nice furniture...and go right on making bets of a size you're comfortable with. The casino manager won't thank you, but your bank account will.

Chapter 8

♠

The Colonel Klink Theory of Decision-Making

Not all gambling happens in casinos, and now we're going to discuss a few tricks that can help you win (or avoid losing, which amounts to the same thing) when confronted with the occasional non-casino gaming opportunity.

Pyramid schemes are one such gamble. The temptation seems easy: Put in $1,000, recruit eight more people at $1,000 each, and you get paid $8,000. The eight people you recruit each have the same chance to earn a $7,000 profit. It works fine, for a *very* short while, but eventually it collapses under its own weight, and the last people in (who are usually your friends, yet another reason to avoid pyramid schemes) get caught holding the bag.

Pyramid schemes are illegal, but for some get-rich-quick dreamers this only adds to the allure. So it was with a mixture of amusement and sadness that I received a phone call from an old buddy: He had been asked into such a scheme, and what did I think of it?

Before I could get up on my soapbox and start lecturing him, though, my buddy added "Joe (not his real name) is already in, but Ace says he thinks it's a bad idea."

Ace is a very smart friend of mine, a good gambler whom I would expect to make the easy correct decision here. Joe is a friend, but he is a terrible gambler who has made all sorts of questionable decisions in his life—a smart guy who somehow keeps getting it wrong.

So I asked my buddy, "Isn't it enough for you to hear that Ace is out and Joe is in?"

"What do you mean?" he asked.

"I mean the fact that Joe thinks this is a good idea should be enough to send you running in the other direction," I said. "Didn't you ever watch Hogan's Heroes on TV?"

"Sure. What about it?"

"Did you ever see the episode where the bomb dropped into the middle of the compound, but didn't go off, and they have to disarm it? And of course none of the Germans knew how, so they asked Hogan."

He didn't recall this particular episode, so I explained that Hogan gets close to finishing disarming the bomb, but eventually finds two wires, and says that cutting one will disarm the bomb, and cutting the other will make it explode, but he doesn't know which is which. So he asks Colonel Klink, who hesitates briefly, and then picks one.

"You're sure?" Hogan asks Klink.

"Yes, definitely," Klink answers. So Hogan starts to cut the wire that Klink picked, and then suddenly, *Snap!*, cuts the other one. And the bomb doesn't go off, of course.

"Why did you ask me," screams Klink, *"if you knew which wire to cut all along?!?"*

"I didn't know which was the right one," smirks Hogan, "but I was sure *you'd* pick the wrong one."

Most of us know someone like Colonel Klink, or my friend Joe...someone well-meaning but who just seems to get it wrong most of the time. When you're confronted with an intriguing gambling proposition, like a pyramid scheme, you can ask a smart friend, but you know as well as I that you're likely to disregard that advice and do what you want.

Instead, I suggest that you ask your Colonel Klink, and if his or her answer matches your inclination, you might just want to rethink things.

Another kind of gambling proposition problem comes up when someone adept at psychology wants you to make a bet on something. This could happen in a bar, around the office water cooler, or in a poker game. The problem arises if this person appears to "have your number," that is, always seems able to get you to pick the wrong side of a bet.

I first encountered this problem in my high school poker game. As sports editor of the high school paper, I had an office with a key-locked door, which was very convenient for poker games. (Who knew that high school was so educational?)

One friend and game regular, Jim Hagney, always had my number. When I should have called his bets, I folded; when I should have folded, I called or raised. At that point in my poker career, Jim knew just what to say to get me to do what he wanted.

Once I realized that Jim had my number, I tried simply tuning him out, ignoring everything he said, and that helped. But I was still wrong more than half the time when we were head to head. So I started flipping a coin, although I never let him see that I was doing this. It just looked like I was playing with my money.

See the reasoning? Jim was simply too much for me back then. Whatever mixture of psychology and reverse psychology he was using almost always had me pointing in the wrong direction. So instead of playing Jim's psychological game, I *changed* the game to one of random chance. At least that way I had a 50-50 chance of being right, which was a heck of a lot better than I'd been doing.

In the long run, if you're going to face down your own personal Jim Hagney, you need to keep studying and improving and figuring out what you're doing wrong, what he's doing right, or both, and I did. I read a lot of poker books during my first year of college (explaining at least in part my "C" in chemistry), and when I returned to my old game that next summer, I recovered all those losses with interest.

In the short run, though, if you find yourself consistently outmaneuvered, don't keep playing the other guy's game. Change the game, change the rules, or introduce some randomizing factor like a coin flip. Fifty-fifty isn't great, but it's a heck of a lot better than I was doing back then, when I looked in the mirror and saw Colonel Klink...staring right back at me.

Chapter 9

♣

The Ultimate in Air Security

I was sitting in my Las Vegas hotel coffee shop exchanging air travel tales with an old gambling buddy (a former professional gambler who now makes roughly 100 times what he used to earn gambling by trading stocks), when I explained, tongue firmly in cheek, why I'm such a calm flier.

"Nothing to worry about anymore," I said. "Ever read *The World According to Garp*, where he buys the house that the airplane crashed into, because the house has already had its disaster and so is now disaster-proof? Well, that's me. I've already survived one plane crash (true story, Eastern Airlines, Atlanta, January 18, 1990), so what are the odds on me ever being in a second one?"

My friend paused to reflect. "Using that theory," he mused, "I suppose you could make sure that you were never the victim of terrorism when you traveled by air. All you would have to do is bring a bomb on board your flight. What would the odds be that *two* people brought a bomb on board the same flight!"

(Editorial Note: Please don't do this or even joke about it at the airport as you will wind up in jail. Now, back to our story.)

We smiled, because we both knew the logical fallacy we were employing. We were pretending that independent events have a cause-and-effect relationship.

Although most rational people recognize that my survival in 1990 does not mean I'm a "specially protected flier" now, many seem to feel that other types of independent events *are* related, such as a roulette ball landing on red three times in a row.

Curiously, different people use this incorrect assumption to draw opposite conclusions. One roulette player might wait around for red to come up three times in a row, and then bet red because red is on a streak. Another player at the same table might wait for the same streak, and then bet *black*, because black is now due.

Go figure.

Actually, both players are making the same mistake, even though the mistake led them to opposite actions. They are assuming that a series of *independent* events makes the next event in the series either more or less likely.

Streaks come in two, and *only* two, kinds. The first occurs when the events in the streak are *dependent* on each other; that is, where an event's occurrence makes it more (or less) likely that it will happen again. The second occurs when the events are *independent* of each other. When you see a chance to make a bet on a dependent streak, grab it. When you see a chance to bet on an independent streak, ignore the streak and examine the bet as a stand-alone event.

Let's look at dependent streaks. What about a baseball winning streak? Sports enthusiasts know that winning is easier when you're confident, and confidence builds when you win. A winning team could have everyone healthy for the first time in a while, have players who like hot weather better, or have discovered a new way to take batting practice. The success isn't random. Reasons exist for the streak, even if they aren't obvious.

What about a salesman who has good and bad days? On the good days he's cheerful and approachable, not desperate because he's already made some sales—he's at the peak of his selling abilities. On the bad days, maybe he's in a bad mood, or desperate because he needs the money—and people can sense the desperation and want no part of it. So this, too, is a dependent streak (and is related to one reason poker players have good and bad days).

Let's look at just what makes something an independent event, or streak. The easiest example is a fair flip of a fair coin. Every time you flip it you have a brand-new result, totally independent of what happened the last time.

Even television has recognized the independent nature of coin flips. A 1998 episode of *Jeopardy* featured a category called "Odds." The first answer was, "The odds of a coin coming up heads if that coin has come up heads 99 times in a row." The correct question, of course, was, "What is Even Money?"

(As a *Jeopardy* exercise, it was clear they were looking for an Even Money "answer," since a contestant couldn't assume a trick coin was being used. Nonetheless, if you or I actually witnessed a coin coming up heads 99 times in a row, we would be foolish if we didn't assume that some kind of trick coin was being used.)

Similarly, if you take a full deck of 52 cards and shuffle them, you have a 50-50 chance of randomly selecting a black card. If you pull a black card, put it back into the deck, shuffle again, and pull again, you will again have a 50-50 chance. The events are, like the fair coin, independent and unrelated.

Now let's change the "pull a black card" game a little. This time, remove the Ace of Spades, lay it aside, and offer to let a friend (who knows the Ace is gone—this is a friendly game) try to pull a black card from the deck at even money. If he pulls a black card, he wins $10. If he pulls a red card, he loses $10.

Congratulations: You are now "the house." Why? Because after you remove the Ace of Spades there are 26 red cards in the deck, and 25 black ones. The odds favor you, because *the second event was dependent on the first one.* Once a black card left the deck, the odds on the game changed. This simple and powerful concept helps explain why blackjack is the one casino game where (given the right conditions and sufficient skill) a few gifted players can beat the house consistently.

Compare the effect of rolling dice or spinning slot machine reels with removing cards from the deck. You aren't changing anything about the dice when you roll them. You aren't wearing out the slot reels. *The previous event has nothing to do with the next one.*

"How can you say that," you ask, "when I've seen some unbelievable streaks, like red coming up 16 times in a row at the roulette table? The mathematical odds against such a streak are enormous—so something must be going on."

You are right. "Something" is going on, but not what you think. Although the odds are against a long streak starting at any given moment, it is a mathematical certainty that long streaks *will* occur over the course of thousands of chances in a week, month, or year.

As a result, people who go to casinos frequently are certain to see some amazing streaks happen. If you play 800 hands of blackjack in a day (easy enough if you play for eight hours at the not-uncommon rate of 100 hands an hour), it would be fantastically *unlikely* not to have a winning streak of five hands in a row at some point. You will also have lots of two-hand streaks, three-hand streaks, and so on.

That these streaks will occur is an inescapable mathematical certainty. The problem is, there's no way to know whether you are in the middle of a long independent streak *until it's over.*

So what does all of this mean for you when you're in Las Vegas?

First and foremost, it means *never* making huge bets, or increasing the size of your bets, when you're in the midst of a losing streak, on the theory that "the streak must end soon." There is no such "must."

Second, it means you must not assume that because you enjoy a fabulous winning streak one day you will do so again. You did not enjoy the streak because you're a magically lucky player. It happened because in the course of a gaming career, such things happen. So do their opposite.

Third, it means not pushing your luck beyond all reason when you're enjoying a hot streak, because there is no guarantee it will continue. Put a little aside, so you have something to show for your streak when it ends, and when the hot streak finally ends, don't chase it with additional big bets because "you were hot." You *were* hot. It's over. Don't give it all back.

To gamble successfully, you need to be able to recognize the difference between non-connected, independent trial events (such as dice-rolling, wheel-spinning, and slot machine reel-spinning) and connected, dependent trial events (such as card games where some cards are visible or have already been dealt).

Any gambling "system" based on assuming that one independent event will affect another independent event is nonsense, pure and simple. Such systems might win for a while, just as playing randomly might win for a while. In the long run they have no impact on your results. Using a "bet red after red comes up three times in a row" system will give you the same 5.26-percent disadvantage as betting red any other time.

When you're gambling outside a casino, where the possibility of cheating exists, then you can be forgiven for considering the possibility that the past might be a good guide to the future. If an unknown backgammon opponent, using his own dice, rolled double sixes three times in a row, I might start to suspect something funny was going on. No less of a gaming expert than James Bond used this suspicion to his advantage in *Octopussy*.

But in a casino, where loaded dice (or the often hoped-for, never found "biased" roulette wheel) are unheard of, your faith in the ability of past independent results to indicate the future can be costly, if it leads you to make bets larger than you would otherwise.

Boiling all of this down to a simple, useful rule, *the trend most important to respect is the one you **don't** want to believe in*, such as a losing streak in poker, craps, slots, sports betting, etc. There's almost always a reason for such streaks, even if you don't know it, so respect trends you dislike! How? Assume it will continue, i.e., you will continue to lose! At that point, you can make a rational decision about whether the pleasure you're getting from gambling is worth the price you're paying.

If you follow that rule, then you can avoid getting hurt without worrying about defining the streak as dependent or independent, and without needing to figure out the reasons for a streak. Naturally this oversimplification won't always be right, and it is still nice to be able to figure out the reasons, for the future of your gaming "career." But in the moment, this simple, easy-to-apply rule will save you from dangerous, expensive losses.

The other side of the very same coin (if you'll pardon the expression) is that if you encounter a trend you *like*, such as a winning streak, be very cautious and lean toward disrespecting it. That is, refuse to take action relying on the streak. In practice, this would mean a thought process like: "I've won three trips in a row. I must be on a winning streak, so next time I'm going to Vegas I'm emptying out the savings account so I can bet really big and win a bundle. Oh, wait a minute, this is a streak I like, so I should be cautious. Okay, I guess I won't bet my life savings after all." Congratulations! You're now using your head for something more important than holding up your hair.

And if you're going to play foolette, I mean *roulette*, go ahead and have fun with your "system." It's no better or worse than any other random bet; just don't have faith in it. If my plane lands safely when next I visit your city, we can talk more about systems then.

Part Three:

Know
Thyself

Chapter 10

◆

The Basics:
Food, Water, and
Rationalizations

The three necessities for life are food, water, and shelter. Of course, for life to be at all fun or meaningful, we need a little more. Some people might list love next, others respect, still others sex. I'm here to maintain that "rationalizations" should make the list at number four.

I doubt I could do a better job of proving the importance of rationalizations than Lawrence Kasdan and Jeff Goldblum did in *The Big Chill*, where to prove the claim that rationalizations are more important than sex, Goldblum asked rhetorically, "Ever go a week without a good rationalization?"

Most gamblers, unfortunately, can't go more than a few *minutes* without a good rationalization. Usually they involve reasons why losing is acceptable.

I've heard a lot of great ones over the years, but I have a favorite—an actual quote from an old poker acquaintance (let's call him Riker) who had been a heavy loser the previous year but who had been doing a little better lately. I mentioned this to him and the following conversation ensued:

"Oh, yeah, I am doing much better this year," Riker agreed. "If you don't count those two games where I dropped three dimes each (a "dime" is $1,000 in gambling parlance), I'm up $500 for the year."

"Um, er, um," I cleverly replied. "Why aren't you counting the $6,000 you lost?"

"Those were weird nights," he said. "One time I was drunk, and the other time I'd just had a big fight with my wife and I was in a crazy mood."

I was younger then and less familiar with this line of reasoning, so I pressed on. "But...you still had to pay the $6,000, right?"

"Sure," he admitted. "I just don't count it in my records."

I decided to drop the matter there. Lessons, as we sometimes snicker in poker games, cost extra. The lesson for Riker: Excuses are just margin notes. Your results are your results, period, end of story.

Why? Because "weird nights" are part of poker and all other forms of gambling. We don't gamble in a vacuum. Sometimes we're in good moods, sometimes we're in bad moods. Sometimes we play with discipline, sometimes we play crazily. Sometimes we even win on the crazy nights, although it's much less likely.

The ability to keep those crazy nights few and far between usually separates the winners from the losers. It almost always separates the big losers from the light losers.

The trick, for people who want to be able to gamble without wrecking their finances, is to lay off the rationalizations. Riker didn't count those bad nights, and so his current self-image was "winning player." That means he might play more poker, and it also means that he's likely to have more three-dime nights, and to keep making excuses for them.

Here are a few other common rationalizations. Take a look and see if you've ever used any of them:

- "It's okay for me to lose for a while, because I'm learning and, in effect, paying for my gambling education. I'll win it all back later when I've learned enough."
- "The other players are much luckier than me."
- "I pretty much broke even" (meaning either that you know you lost and don't want to admit it, or you were pretty sure you were losing so you didn't keep track).
- "I lost but the casino gave me so much free stuff that I pretty much broke even" (see above).

Some, perhaps even most, players rationalize without even realizing it. I once traveled to Las Vegas with a friend who won a $250 slot jackpot early in the trip. Over the rest of the trip she lost about $300, so she wound up a net $50 loser. But when asked about her trip later, she would invariably say, "I won $250!"

Obviously she *did* win $250, so the statement was the truth, although an incomplete truth. It's easy to see how someone could focus on a vivid jackpot memory as the trip result, and not want to think about the rest of the trip. Why not just brush those gradual losses away like crumbs on a tablecloth, something not worthy of notice? It's nice to be able to think of yourself as a winner, or of your trip as a winning trip.

But this sort of thinking can get in the way of improved results the next time around. If your memory or self-image is, instead, the real "I won a $250 jackpot but gave it back over the next couple of days," perhaps after the next jackpot you'll resolve to bring some of it home, and thus go home a *real* winner, instead of a pretend winner.

In this particular example, the real truth wasn't so bad. What's wrong with saying "I won a jackpot early and so I had three days of fun in Las Vegas and it only cost $50?" Not a darn thing. I don't think there's anything wrong with losing a *reasonable* amount, as long as you can afford it and it bears a rational relationship to the amount of fun or entertainment you had playing.

But because we're taught that losing is bad, losing is wrong, a lot of us will do or say *anything* to avoid facing or admitting the truth. Once you start to go down that road, more harmful rationalizations are that much closer.

I could go on, but you can see how people who want to gamble can find almost any excuse to keep going. I worry about people when they rationalize, because that's when they can get hurt. As long as you can look your results in the eye, keep good records, and face the truth head-on, gambling can be fun, and you will be able to make good decisions.

Rationalizations, though, are the children of losing, and they breed true, creating more losing. Tell yourself the truth, no matter how uncomfortable, and you'll live to play another day.

Chapter 11

♥

Are You 90% Sure?

In this chapter we're going to look at a fun little test with which you can dazzle and impress your friends. My purpose, though, is to see if you have a good feel for the amount of risk you might be taking in a given situation.

If you have that feel, trading stocks, betting on sports (with odds, not pointspreads), and playing poker are all gambling pastimes for which you have potential. If you don't, those kinds of gambling are probably too risky for you, and indeed any kind of "make up a proposition and bet it on the spot" betting is probably not such a hot idea, either.

The test was originally created by a stock trading firm to test potential floor traders. The idea was to see if applicants understood the difference between playing it safe, and playing it *too* safe. The firm wanted people who could understand when they were taking a modest risk.

I'm going to ask you 10 questions, and your assignment is to state a range within which you feel *90-percent certain* that you are answering the question correctly. Put another way, you have to be sure enough to be willing to make a bet with a friend where you won $10 if you were right, but lost $90 if you were wrong.

Obviously you have to be pretty darn sure to bet at odds like that, but, at the same time, if you're too conservative in selecting your range, your friend won't even be willing to risk the $10. Let's apply this to an example: How many beers are consumed per year by the average male American college student?

If you were to create a range where you were 100-percent certain you were right, you might say "between 1 and 2,000." And while such an answer would be correct, it would be *too* correct, that is, too conservative: Your friend would never risk $10 against a mere $90 with such a range, because his only chance to win would be if the average male college student drank more than 2,000 beers a year (roughly a six pack *every* day) and that just isn't true.

Your goal is to achieve exactly 90-percent accuracy, so a better guess might be "between 4 and 400." It is *conceivable* the answer lies outside those numbers, but very likely not. With a range of 4 to 400, your friend might be willing to risk his $10.

Thus the scoring is unlike any test you've ever taken— because a "perfect" score (10 out of 10) is not as good an effort as scoring 8 or 9 out of 10! On the other hand, if you only get seven or fewer right, you're taking too great a risk (which means you're someone who is willing to accept too small a payoff for the risk you're taking—not a good characteristic for a gambler).

The questions, as you observed in the example, are matters that most people would not be expected to know. If you do know an answer, the range you pick should be quite small.

Remember, you are trying to take a tiny risk: you're not shooting for perfect accuracy. On the other hand, if you're really clueless about a question, protect yourself with a wide range, as you'll see that I did in several of my answers. Write your answers down, in the form of a range, and let's see what happens:

♥

1. The weight, in pounds, of a Boeing 747.

2. The distance, in miles, between New York and Tokyo.

3. The population of Nigeria in 1995.

4. The number of books in the New Testament.

5. The number of seats on the Chicago Board of Trade.

6. The mean average high temperature in San Jose, Costa Rica, in June.

7. The number of rebounds collected by Wilt Chamberlain in his NBA career.

8. The percentage of the U.S. population living below the poverty line in 1995.

9. The number of electoral votes collected by Bill Clinton in 1992.

10. The number of consecutive matches Andy Glazer had to win to capture the kickoff tournament at the 1985 World Amateur Backgammon Championships.

♥

Okay, get cracking, and be sure to finish the test before you read the answers.

The real answers:
1. 396,000
2. 0,751
3. 98 million
4. 30
5. 3,661
6. 77
7. 23,800
8. 14.1%
9. 374
10. 9

The answers I gave:
1. 100,000-7,500,000
2. 8,000-12,000
3. 3-115 million
4. 4-34
5. 150-3,500
6. 70-86
7. 20,000-40,000
8. 10%-25%
9. 250-500
10. 0-20 (A different question was used when I took the test, the answer to which was 11.)

As you can see when I took the test I scored 8 out of 10, which impressed my trader friend. A good score isn't merely getting 8 or 9 right; it's also having most of the right answers fall comfortably within the range you set, or the wrong answers to be near misses. I knew I didn't have a good grip on airplane weights, so I gave myself a wide margin for error. I'd been to Costa Rica and knew about the surprisingly cool climate, so I didn't need a range up into the 90s.

So now that you've taken the test yourself, and scored your results, let's evaluate what they mean for your pursuit of gambling as a hobby:

- ♥ **10 out of 10**: You like to win, which is good, but you're very conservative. In fact you're so conservative that you're probably not reading this book, because you would never consider gambling. Good for you. Just make sure that when you're 85 years old and looking back at your life, you don't regret having not taken a risk now and then.

- ♥ **8 or 9 out of 10:** A winner! You have a terrific feel for what a small degree of risk means. You probably gamble well, or have the potential to do so, and you probably were pretty good at math back in school, too.

- ♥ **6 or 7 out of 10:** Not great, but certainly not bad either. If your correct guesses were very comfortably in the middle of a range, or if your incorrect guesses were very near misses, so much the better. You have a decent feel for odds, no question, but probably have a slight tendency to take too much risk. If you stay aware of that, you probably won't get hurt.

- ♥ **4 or 5 out of 10.** Hmmm…let's hope you didn't really understand what I wanted you to do on the test. A score of 4 or 5 means you are a risk-taker, someone who likes living close to the edge; either that, or you just don't have a good feel for what being very certain means. This makes you vulnerable to bad bets in bars or at the office, and might mean you're too willing to take the casino on at some of the bad-odds games, like the money wheel or keno. And you're spending too much on lottery tickets.

- ♥ **3 or less.** Harumph! Read what I wrote for "4 or 5 out of 10" and put some teeth in it. You're almost certainly too much of an optimist to gamble successfully.

Hey, there's nothing wrong with that: You can lead an awfully happy life without ever going near a casino. But if you do walk into one, you'll probably lose. Keep reading, come to a seminar, or play for very low stakes, infrequently.

I hope you now you have a little clearer self-image as far as your gambling potential, though you certainly should not consider this one test conclusive. Whether you got nine right or two right, it's just one indicator.

I want to repeat and emphasize that there is nothing at all wrong with being someone who's not too good at gambling...as long as you don't gamble! If you enjoy gambling, and your score wasn't what you'd hoped, keep reading. You'll improve rapidly—at least, I'm 90-percent sure that you will.

Chapter 12

♠

$\$=MC^2$:
Glazer's Theory
of Relativity

Money, like time, is relative. Is $400 a lot of money? When you're buying a house, the difference between $220,000 and $220,400 seems irrelevant. When you're buying a car, the difference between $22,000 or $22,400 doesn't seem like much, if you like the car. But when you're buying a pack of chewing gum, the difference between prices of 50¢ and $400.50 matters a great deal, no matter how much you like the gum.

Although it's the exact same $400 in all three cases, our willingness to pay it varies dramatically, because in the first case it seems tiny relative to the size of the transaction, and in the last it seems monumental relative to it.

The same effect occurs in casinos, sometimes with devastating consequences for players having off nights.

A lot of people who gamble at all sorts of games have reasonable trip after reasonable trip, losing a little here, winning a little there, generally having a good time of it. And then, *Wham!*, they have one night where the wheels just come off the wagon. They start losing, start doubling up to catch up, and before they know it, they're in the hole for six month's salary.

How, why, and when does this happen? The kind of emotional circumstances that leave you vulnerable to meltdowns are limitless, but most meltdowns share one characteristic: At some point, after you've lost some significant amount, you reach a point of what I call "misery indifference." That is, you're already so upset, already so far in the hole, that another few hundred or few thousand dollars seems irrelevant...right then.

For example, suppose your gambling loss comfort level is $500 for a night (it might be $5 or $50,000; I'm just using $500 as an example). You certainly don't want to lose that much, but you've lost that much before and you expect it will probably happen again. It's the price you pay for those nights when you win $500, and you have plenty of those, too. You can still play rationally when down $500; your emotions aren't overwhelming you.

Now suppose you somehow find yourself down not $500, but $2,000. Maybe it happened because you had a few drinks, maybe you were upset about something, maybe you were just incredibly unlucky. The reason you lost $2,000 doesn't matter for purposes of *this* discussion, although it certainly does matter.

How do you feel, down $2,000? Your head is probably swimming. You're angry. You're miserable. You're depressed. You're not rational. You feel like a knucklehead. In fact you're probably experiencing most of the better-known negative emotions all at once. You're about as unhappy as you can be, and that means that you're in big, big trouble if you keep on gambling.

Why? When you're already down $2,000, and previously a big winning or losing night for you was a quarter of that, another $2,000 seems irrelevant. Down $2,000, down

$4,000, what's the difference? You're buried and miserable *either way.*

The difference, as you have no doubt already calculated, is $2,000, and although it feels like *nothing* then and there, the next day it's going to feel like—$2,000.

We all have strong moments and weak moments, we all have good days and bad days. The trick, for both the professional and amateur gambler, is to make sure that the bad days don't ruin six months of otherwise decent results.

So if you ever find yourself in the middle of a really bad night, and thinking that you don't care about getting further in the hole...congratulations! You've found *exactly* the right time to leave, and leave fast.

Sure, you won't make a dramatic comeback that way. But you almost certainly weren't going to do that anyway. Very few players play better or think more clearly when they're stuck a bundle. A lot of players improve when they're down a little bit, because they grow more conservative, and they were too free and easy to start out. But the psychology differs when you're buried deep.

You don't have to be a genius to recognize "misery indifference" when you've reached it. If phrases like "don't care," "who cares," or "I deserve it" start drifting in and out of your mind, you're there. The tough part, and the part that separates people who can gamble as a hobby from those who shouldn't, is having the strength to stand up and call it a night. A *lot* of people can't or, more accurately, won't.

Because you are almost certainly not thinking clearly when you hit your point of misery indifference, following my advice and leaving is hard to do, even if you remember the advice. You're too busy shouting at yourself: "I'm getting the money back! My bad luck can't possibly last! I played smart and look where it got me! Well now I'm playing *angry!*"

Whew! Sounds like it's going to be tough for the voice of reason to sneak in there, doesn't it? Any kind of break you can talk yourself into, even 10 minutes, will be a big help. Even if you decide to go back in after the 10 minutes, the short break will probably help, and when you continue losing, you'll later have a natural point to look back at and say, "Why didn't I leave when I knew I should?"

Most people have to learn this lesson the hard way at least once. Until you've felt the insanity of those big-loss emotions, you can't be expected to predict your reactions. But once you've had a chance to pull out the old retro-specto-scope, and look back regretfully at your behavior, you have a much better chance to avoid a repetition.

If just *one time* you can get to that point of fury and do the right thing by leaving, you will have made a huge breakthrough, because the next day, even though you will feel bad about the big loss, you'll feel a mature satisfaction that it didn't turn into a disaster. From then on, you'll find it much easier to leave in the nick of time. You'll feel smart, and you'll want to feel smart again.

So that's my request to you. When you feel yourself choked by the raging negative emotions of a big loss, just get out *one time*. Tell yourself it's an experiment. If you have to access a negative emotion to function, tell yourself you don't deserve the right to play anymore. Tell yourself *anything* you can, and if it gets you home, I promise, you'll feel awfully good about it the next day.

Leaving the casino before a really bad night becomes an unmitigated disaster is one important part of long-term gambling health. But it was still a really bad night, and you can take steps to avoid its repetition.

If you do have a really bad night, don't come up with a good rationalization. Accept it for what it was, and add a footnote to your self-image: "Capable of meltdown under following circumstances." Then if you see some of those circumstances surfacing again, get the heck out of Dodge. Better yet, don't even go to Dodge.

There are four paths to become a winning gambler: The two obvious ones are winning more on your winning nights, and having more winning nights. The two less obvious (and perhaps more important) ones are losing less on your losing nights, and having fewer losing nights. It all adds up, and it all counts. If you can avoid the really bad nights, when the end of the year comes around, you might have enough left to buy a car...instead of a pack of gum.

Chapter 13

♣

Ready,
Fire, Aim!

It's about 3 p.m. on Friday, and your pulse rate is starting to rise, because you're taking the 6:55 flight to Las Vegas for a weekend of gambling, shows, action, and adventure.

I contend that if you spend a little of the intervening time thinking about just what you want out of that trip (I mean, you're not really going to be thinking about *work* between 3 and 5 on a Friday anyway, right?), you will be much more likely to achieve your goal.

You've probably heard old sayings like, "It's easier to hit a target if you aim at it," or, "People don't plan to fail, they fail to plan." Planning and aiming don't seem to happen much in the gaming world. If you set a loss budget and call ahead to check on shows, you're probably in the top 5 percent of gaming planners, but there's much more you could be thinking about.

To me, the big questions are, "What excites me about a gambling trip while it's happening?" and "What kind of result do I want from the trip?" The answers to these questions are usually less obvious than most people realize.

Let's start with the result you want from the trip. Just about everyone will say, "I want to win," but that's not enough. It fails as a plan for the same reason that a job search based on "I want to make $40,000 a year" is almost certainly doomed to failure. It's too vague.

Sure you want to win, but how much? For many people, as long as they have a winning trip, the actual amount won isn't too important: They just like the feeling of coming home a winner, of being able to tell their friends they won. Sure they'd rather win $1,000 than $100, but given a choice of the two series of trips listed here, this kind of person would be much happier with the first than the second:

5-trip series 1: Lots of small wins, one big loss:
Trip 1. Won $100
Trip 2. Won $150
Trip 3. **Lost $600**
Trip 4. Won $100
Trip 5. Won $150
(Net result: lost $100)

5-trip series 2: Lots of small losses, one big win:
Trip 1. Lost $100
Trip 2. Lost $200
Trip 3. **Won $600**
Trip 4. Lost $100
Trip 5. Lost $100
(Net result: won $100)

To this person, the actual cash result isn't as important as feeling like a winner four times out of five. Of course, change the Trip 3 results to winning or losing six *thousand* dollars instead of six hundred, and probably even the most "want that winning feeling" kind of person would pick series number 2 (a net $5,600 winner instead of net $5,600 loser).

Very nice and very theoretical, you might say. How can this "choice" mean anything when it's impossible to create casino results in advance? If I could choose to win or lose I would always choose winning!

Of course we would all choose winning, but I'm not talking about choosing between winning and losing over the long run, but rather about having winning sessions and losing sessions.

One way to do that is by using "session betting." You play until either you've won $100 or lost *twice* that amount. Unless you are a really terrible gambler, the mathematical laws governing fluctuations dictate that by using this approach you'll have more winning sessions than losing sessions, because in the roller coaster of casino ups and downs, it's easier to win $100 than it is to lose $200.

The downside is that when you *do* lose, you lose twice as much, and so you're *not* changing your long-term results with session betting; you're just altering the ebb and flow of the money a little. Nonetheless, you walk out of a casino feeling like a winner more often than feeling like a loser, and for some people, that's very attractive.

Let's take another example. Suppose that your goal for a Vegas trip is to win $1,000, and that nothing else matters, not how much fun you have, not what game you play, and so on—and that it is okay with you if you lose $1,000 because tomorrow the mortgage payment is due and if you don't have $2,000 it doesn't matter if you have $1,000.

Granted, that's a pretty specific and unusual set of circumstances (though actually not so far removed from how Fred Smith, the founder of Federal Express, saved his company in its early days with a Vegas trip). But if those were your circumstances, the correct strategy would be very clear: Go make one $1,000 bet at a game with the lowest possible house percentage.

Probably that would be a $1,000 bet on Bank in baccarat, although there is an interesting craps strategy you could try, too (the details are a more advanced lesson for another day).

Why one bet? Because house percentages work best when the casino gets lots and lots of chances at your money. That's why small-limit casinos are called "grind joints," because over time and at small limits they eventually grind your bankroll down to nothing.

If the house gets only one shot at your money with a 2-percent advantage, 51 times out of 100 the house will win, and 49 times out of 100 you will win—very easy odds to live with. But if the house gets several thousand cracks at you, that small edge will eventually grind you down, effectively reducing your chance of winning not to 49 percent, but to zero.

The grind effect thus plays a big part in your trip planning. If your primary goal is to come home a winner, you need to make fewer bets. If your goal is lots of betting action, you need to set a loss limit, and not be too disappointed if you don't come home a winner.

The grind effect and your personal motivation for a gambling trip are important aspects of *Casino Gambling the Smart Way*, and we're not done with them yet. If the idea of Ready, Aim, Fire! makes more sense to you than Ready, Fire, Aim!, keep reading.

Chapter 14

◆

(Per)Cents and Sensibility

In Chapter 13 we discussed the grind effect: how small house percentages don't mean much when making just one or two bets, but how they become overwhelming obstacles when making thousands of bets. We're going to expand on that idea now.

Because I prefer my readers to stay with me instead of running away screaming in terror, I usually stay away from heavy math. If you're willing to take the math on faith, normally I can explain the key concept(s) without evoking painful memories of the SAT exam.

Come back here! I didn't say I was going to get into heavy math now. Just a teeny, tiny bit, about as painful as a flu shot (which is a heck of a lot less painful than the flu).

You've seen the signs: "Loose slots, 98% payback." Or maybe you've read that roulette has a 5.26-percent house edge, or that the house edge on craps Pass Line bets is 1.41-percent.

What do these numbers mean? Some people think that they are predictions of what happens to your bankroll in a gaming weekend. In other words, barring unusually good luck or bad luck, if you start with $1,000, and play 98-percent return slots for the weekend, you would wind up with ₵080.

Nope.

The key to understanding house percentages is that they apply each and every time you make a bet. They're a little like the casino's version of compound interest. They mean that you stand to lose a little bit each time you bet, although of course that's not what happens.

Let's use roulette as the first example: When you bet $10 on black or red, the house pays you even money. So even though you face a house percentage of 5.26 percent, you don't wind up with $9.48 after the wheel stops. You wind up with either $20 or $0. The percentage kicks in because if you play enough times, on the *average* you will lose a few cents (48¢, to be precise) each time. This happens because of those green "0" and "00" slots, where bets on red *and* black lose.

So what happens when you bet $10 per roulette spin for a few hours? With average luck after 100 spins you would rate to lose not 48¢, but $48 (actually $47.74...and of course if you've been making $10 bets, that won't be the real number. Probably you'll be down $50, maybe $40 or $60).

What if instead of roulette spins, you'd been playing craps, and just betting $10 on the Pass Line each time? After 100 rolls (actually 100 *results*, not rolls, because when you bet the Pass Line, a lot of the rolls mean nothing to your bet), average luck would mean you were losing $14.10.

So in trying to figure out how the percentages are going to affect you, you need to know three things: the percentage (available from me or any gaming book); the size of your average bet; and (here's the big one) the number of bets you're going to make.

Games proceed at different paces. Blackjack moves very fast if you're head-to-head with the dealer, and a lot slower if you're at a table filled with social players. Craps moves pretty slowly if the table is full and all you're doing is betting the Pass Line. It also can be a little boring, which is why they fill the table with all those other instant gratification bets, which carry much heavier house percentages! The pace of roulette isn't dizzying, but watching that ball spin is.

The fastest game in town? You know the answer—those slots you love. Especially now that you can feed in bills and just press a button to "play max coins" and "spin reels." A frenzied slot player can get in hundreds of spins per hour, and each time the house is taking its teeny-tiny bite.

Piranha fish take teeny tiny bites, too, but put enough of them in the water and you have a horror movie.

The lesson? First, breathe a little, especially if you're playing a game where you control the pace, like slots. You can play for two days at a leisurely pace with the same expected loss as one day at high speed.

When playing craps, stick to a Pass Line bet (as small as possible in relation to your odds bet), which will provide natural pauses in the action. You're still gambling, you're still playing your game of choice, you can still feel the adrenaline flow. But by making fewer total bets, your chances of winning will be vastly improved, and you won't lose nearly as often.

The second lesson is tougher: Bad percentage games and bets really chew up your bankroll in a hurry. I call this a tough lesson because probably you have a game you like to play, and you're not anxious to change it. But the reality is that making thousands of bets at a game with a 5-percent or greater disadvantage leaves you virtually no chance whatsoever of coming out a weekend winner.

When you have a winning trip, you've been a little lucky. It's certainly not impossible for that to happen, but it's enormously more likely to happen when you're bucking a light percentage (1.5 percent or less) than a heavy one. By playing sensibly, those tiny casino bites of a few cents at a time won't overwhelm you the way the bigger bites of heavier house percentages would.

So you have to examine your motivation for a gambling trip. If you want lots and lots of action—a lot of hours at a fast betting pace—you can have that, as long as you're willing to accept a loss. If you want a winning trip, you can (occasionally) have that, if you're willing to stick to certain kinds of games, play fewer hours, and employ a more leisurely betting pace.

No lectures here on which approach is better. As long as you understand what's going on, you can make the right choice—for you. In Chapter 15, we'll move away from the numbers, and look at some of the psychological aspects of your choice.

Chapter 15

♥

Without Questions, There Are No Answers

Because understanding your motivation for a gambling trip makes it more likely that you will have a successful trip, according to your own *personal* definition of success, here's a short multiple-choice test for which there are no right answers—only answers that are right for you, and recognition of which will help you enjoy your trip more:

♥

1. I go to Las Vegas so that I can
   a. spend every possible minute gambling.
   b. soak in the whole casino experience—gaming, shows, people-watching.
   c. be someone that I'm not the rest of the year.
   d. fantasize about winning lots of money.
   e. win lots of money.
   f. feel like I'm in control.
   g. feel like I'm out of control.

2. I consider that I had a successful trip to Vegas if I
   a. win a lot.
   b. win anything.
   c. break even.
   d. don't lose much.
   e. just lose the cash I brought with me and don't go get cash advances.
   f. got in plenty of action and adventure; the financial outcome isn't important.
   g. get comped for my room, food, and shows and get treated like a big shot.

3. I think I would have the most fun if I
   a. made a few really big, hold-my-breath-size bets.
   b. played for a long time.
   c. beat the casino at its own game by taking advantage of deals and coupons.

♥

Once you've answered these questions (and it will take a lot of honest self-analysis to do so), you can fine-tune your approach to your trip so that you succeed according to *your* definition of success. A full discussion of how to fine-tune and succeed could fill a book or a seminar, but we can scratch the surface here.

Question 1 displays some of the many different, valid approaches available. If you want to spend a lot of hours at the tables, you probably need to be willing to lose a fairly large sum, or to play for very low limits. A goal of lots of hours at high limits with no losses is totally unrealistic, so you need to make a choice *before* you get on the plane.

If you want to soak in the whole casino experience, you shouldn't be trying to earn comps, which forces you to play a lot in one hotel.

If being someone else does it for you, then maybe part of your budget should go for fancy clothes, and you should tip big for front-row show seats.

If merely *fantasizing* about winning a large sum floats your boat, you can do that much more inexpensively at keno than at slots, because of keno's very slow pace. If you hate the idea of paying that huge house keno percentage (and you should!), or if you find sitting around just playing keno incredibly boring (and I would), try the slots; they're better than table games for big-score fantasizing.

If you actually want to win over the long haul, you probably need to learn a simple blackjack card counting system and be willing to move from casino to casino a lot. You can come close by finding a craps table offering un-limited odds, but even these low-disadvantage situations mean eventual defeat. A great poker player can win in the long run too, but most players are a lot less great than they think, and the educational process to achieve true greatness is lengthy and usually expensive.

Question 2 begins to look at money management. If you want to win a lot, stopping when you've won $200 is silly; if you want to come home a winner and the amount isn't as important, a rat-holing system where you stash some chips after winning makes sense. If you want to avoid cash advances, leave your checks and credit cards at home! If big action and comps are your style, and you're willing to absorb big losses, you can have fun *if* you do it with your eyes open and aren't kidding yourself about what's likely to happen.

Question 3 gets at both your motivation and your self-discipline. If you have a budget of $100 a day, you can spread that into a lot of little bets, or you can take a shot at playing with black chips (okay, *one* black chip). Most of the time you'll lose, of course, but once in a while you'll be able to turn $100 into $1,000 or more.

The "el cheapo" coupon and promotion vacation isn't for me, but I know plenty of people who love to "take advantage" of casinos this way. It's a game within a game.

The common thread that runs through all of these questions and answers is the extreme importance of both understanding yourself and being honest with yourself. Fib to your friends about your results if you must (though consider that by inventing false stories of success, you might be luring someone into a false sense of security or optimism and, hence, be partially to blame for the losses they incur), but *to thine own self be true.*

If you can't do that or won't do that, casino gambling is a very dangerous hobby, and if it's getting out of control, you might want to consider calling your local chapter of Gambler's Anonymous or 1-800-GAMBLER. If you can be honest with yourself, casino gambling can be lots of fun.

By taking the time to assess yourself and what you want out of your trip, you greatly increase your chances of having a good trip. But until you've asked yourself the right questions, you can't hope to have the right answers.

Chapter 16

♠

To Maintain Your Power, Don't Drive for an Hour

I've heard a lot of people say that they couldn't live in Las Vegas, or indeed any casino town, because the easy temptation of games so close by would be too hard to resist, and for people who gamble more than they should, that's a good insight.

The explosive growth of casino gambling, not just in Las Vegas and Atlantic City but throughout the country, means that quite a few more people now live very close to casinos, increasing the potential for indulging momentary weakness.

I don't see a good way out of that box if a casino opens up next door. I mean, if you live in Vicksburg, Mississippi, and you know you gamble more than you should, do you move out of town when they put up the riverboats? If the problem is severe enough, maybe, but that's not a realistic option for most people.

Instead, if you now find yourself living close to a casino, you just need to buckle down and follow the advice offered throughout this book even more, because you'll probably be gambling more, and the more you gamble, the more the house percentages will eat away your bankroll.

There's a secondary problem to all this casino growth, one that many people in the New York metro area discovered when Atlantic City suddenly became a relatively easy drive: how to gamble intelligently when you've driven to a casino just for the day or evening, when you're not planning on a long trip, and not getting a room.

When you're in Las Vegas for three days, it's relatively easy to quit for the night when you hit a losing streak: You know you can get 'em the next day. But if your drive to the casino takes an hour or two, and you're planning on returning home the same day, you're putting yourself in a very dangerous position—because the "investment" of all that driving time makes it very unlikely that you'll be willing to turn around and go home if you start off badly.

For example, one time when I was living in Carmel, California, I drove to one of my favorite poker clubs, Bay 101 in San Jose, a drive of, you guessed it, one hour. After about two hours of play it had become clear that Lady Luck wasn't going to be smiling on me that night. If the game had been held 10 minutes from home, I'd have left, knowing that I could return anytime I wanted. But I already had an hour of drive time invested in this trip and it would be an hour driving home—a lot of effort for a short game.

So I decided to buck my instincts and keep playing, and about the only thing I got right was my assessment that Lady Luck wasn't smiling on me that night. Several hours and several hundred dollars later, having finally gotten my "money's worth" out of the drive, I went home.

Driving back to Carmel, it all became clear: I had put myself in a situation where it was too hard to leave. I was doing the very opposite of "Float Like a Butterfly, Sting

Like a Bee" (see Chapter 1). "Physician," I thought, "heal thyself!"

Paradoxically, had I been living next door to Bay 101, leaving would have been a snap, because returning would have been trivially easy. But living at a "safer" distance, I was faced with a more difficult choice.

I'm not suggesting that if you like to gamble and live an hour from the nearest casino that you move closer—that's giving gambling an awfully high priority (it's a coincidence that I now live 15 minutes from Bay 101). Instead, recognize the inherent danger in those middle distances, and give yourself an out.

One kind of "out" is to plan ahead for something else fun to do in the casino town, something enjoyable enough to tempt you to leave the tables. It might be a show you've wanted to see, or a friend who lives nearby—any kind of treat that makes it easier to punt when the action isn't favoring you. It's especially good if your alternative is something you've been wanting to do for a while but haven't gotten around to it. If your gambling experience is terrific, your backup plan is easy to resist. If your gambling experience is less than terrific, you have a built-in lure to get you out of the casino, beyond your mere self-control, which as most gamblers know doesn't always work perfectly when needed.

If your backup plan involves getting together with friends, you'll probably need to explain the situation to them and have some understanding friends. "Hi, Suzanne, this is Andy. I'd like to come hang out for a while tonight if my gambling isn't going well. If the gambling goes well I won't show up." Suzanne would have to be a pretty accommodating friend, especially since you're not likely to arrive in the best of moods.

Nonetheless, most of us do have some accommodating friends, or at least can, with a little creativity, come up with a good Plan B (in advance!) in case the gambling goes awry. But you definitely need to work it out ahead of time: When you're steamed from losing, you're not thinking clearly enough to come up with a good escape route.

Of course, the simplest way out of *any* trap is to avoid walking into it at all. If you find the "one-hour drive" dilemma causes frequent problems, you're probably better off skipping the local casinos and saving your gambling for Las Vegas. The cost of the airfare and room might be cheap in comparison to a night on the town when Lady Luck is escorting someone else.

♣♦♥♠

Part Four:

A Winning Frame of Mind

Chapter 17

♣

The Big Score,
Part One:
The Lottery

Most gamblers dream of someday striking it rich, of making The Big Score, or at least winning enough money to make a difference in lifestyle—enough for a nice new car, say.

And while I advocate sensible play, there's nothing at all wrong with dreaming about a Big Score, or going one step further and trying to hit one, as long as you don't make lots of bad percentage bets or throw away small wins recklessly in pursuit of it.

So let's look at ways you might reasonably (or unreasonably) try for The Big Score, and examine some of the risks and psychologies of each approach.

Playing a state lottery is by far the most common method. It only costs a dollar, you can buy tickets practically anywhere, and if you win there's a built-in defense against blowing it foolishly, because you get paid not in one chunk but over 20 years.

That said, lotteries are such poor gaming risks that no casino commission would let a casino get away with running one (while the odds on winning the big jackpot on some of the new slot machines are actually tougher than winning a lottery, the smaller "in-between-jackpot" payoffs these machines offer still make them better gambles than lotteries).

Let's use the California lottery as an example. The odds against winning are 18,040,000 to 1, a number much too large to mean anything to most people, especially when we all watched Captain Kirk triumph over million-to-one odds every week.

With odds of 18 million to one, you might figure that for the lottery to be a good gamble, the pool would have to build up to a prize of more than $18 million, which happens occasionally. Actually it has to go much higher. Let's say the payoff is $20 million. Because you get paid over 20 years, you receive $1 million a year. But the million you'll get paid in year 20 isn't worth a million dollars now. Because of inflation, it's worth a lot less. You also have to further adjust the payoff for the taxes you'll have to pay.

When you crank these two items in, it turns out that the California lottery would be a "good gamble" only if the prize pool were more like $70 million...and even then only if you could be guaranteed of winning the whole thing, and you can't—the big pools are usually split, because so many tickets are purchased. So most of the time when you buy a lottery ticket in California you're getting paid $3 million when you should be getting paid more than $70 million. Not a very good gamble, odds-wise.

So what, you say, if you only get paid $3 million? You're still happy, because $3 million still changes your life dramatically. And, heck, it's only a dollar, so relax, will you?

Well, if it were only one dollar, I would relax, but of course it isn't. At a dollar a week, it's $52 a year. At $10 a week, it's $520 a year...and suddenly you're playing with real money.

Now, if you have the self-discipline to play only a dollar a week, maybe playing Lotto makes sense, because for $52 you have purchased a one-year right to dream about being a millionaire. The key is to realize that it's pretty much the same dream if you play $1 a week or $10 a week...a dream that almost certainly is not going to come true. But in one case, you're spending $52 to dream, and in the other, you're spending $520 to dream. I don't know about you but I'd rather use the other $468 to go to the Bahamas.

Sadly, some people spend much more than $10 a week. I read about one midwestern couple who sold their home when the lottery first came to their state, so that they could buy 34,000 tickets. They reasoned that in buying 34,000 tickets, they would have a better chance than anyone else to win, and they were right—a *better* chance, but still a terribly poor one, which is what they were after the drawing: terribly poor.

Although you might think "those pathetic folks got what they deserved," recognize that they merely represent the extreme of what all multiple ticket players are doing: spending too much for the right to dream about The Big Score.

You buy the right to dream with the *first* ticket. After that, you're just making bad bets.

By the way, if you're one of the many people who buy lottery tickets to give some higher power the chance to reward you for being good, I've got two points for you to consider:

First, if God wants you to win, buying just one ticket should be enough. Second, in most religions, God is considered both all-knowing and all-powerful. So if your god wants you to be rich, I'm sure he or she is plenty smart enough to figure out a way to do it, *without* requiring you to buy lottery tickets.

The odds on the smaller lottery games are horrible, too. A Pick Three pays 500-1, but the odds are 1,000-1. Pick Three is a state's way of taking over the old "numbers racket." Except that in most places, winning via a numbers runner pays 700-1. So the criminals that the states are supposedly trying to supplant with Pick Three are offering better odds. No wonder crime doesn't pay.

Worse still, the people buying Pick Three often can't afford it. I have watched men who had obviously just gotten paid buying 50 of the darn things, "investing" perhaps a third or a quarter of their meager paychecks in as dubious a scheme as Jackie Gleason's Ralph Cramden character ever tried. It's heartbreaking to watch—no joke.

As to Scratchers (the cardboard tickets where you scratch off a coating with a coin), boy, now we're *really* talking about getting hosed. Not only are the odds and payoffs terrible, but the dream you're buying lasts only a few seconds. At least with Lotto you can dream for a few days, or with Pick Three for a few hours. With Scratchers, you dream for a few seconds, get that silvery junk all over your fingers and clothes, and then like a good lab rat you press the food pellet button again. Yuuch!

So why gamble with the state? Only one reason—it's easy. The tickets are everywhere, an easy lure for your change. It's only a dollar here, a dollar there. So here's my challenge: Add up how much you actually spend on Lotto, Pick Three, Scratchers, and all such state rip-offs. Most regular players will be surprised how much it adds up to in the course of a year. There are better ways to pursue The Big Score, and we'll talk about them next time.

Chapter 18

♦

The Big Score, Part Two: Realistic Longshots

We talked about lotteries in Chapter 17, and the chance of hitting The Big Score against odds of 18 million to one. Here's a little perspective on that number for you.

If you live to be 80 years old, you live for 29,220 days. So something that is so unusual that it happens only one day out of your whole life is only 29,220:1 against. You would have to live 617 such lifetimes to live 18 million days, so unless you are Duncan MacLeod of the Clan Mac-Leod (you know, the immortal sword-wielding *Highlander* guy), you're probably not going to live long enough to catch an 18 million to one shot.

Does that mean you should abandon hope of The Big Score? Not necessarily. First of all, we established last time that if you limit your lottery play to a dollar a week, you buy the right to dream for only $52 a year, which is a not unreasonable investment.

There are also lots of Big Scores available at odds shorter than 18 million to one. Because there's a direct relationship between the odds and the payoff (higher odds equals bigger payoff), your first question is, what do you really want? Do you want a scheme that actually gives you a chance to hit? If so, you probably need to set your sights on a Sort of Big Score. If, on the other hand, you mostly want to be able to dream, Lotto works just fine.

Almost all forms of Big Score betting charge you a premium for scoring big all at once. Keno is a good example—it's very similar to a lottery, although the maximum payoff is much lower than a lottery, usually somewhere between $50,000 and $250,000.

The best way to play Keno (a phrase which to me isn't all that different from "the best way to get food poisoning"...and come to think of it Keno is often played in restaurants) is to play the minimum number of spots which offer a big jackpot. If you can win a big jackpot by hitting 10 out of 10 spots, don't play 15 spots just because there are payoffs for hitting 14 out of 15. It's still a bad gamble, but played one ticket at a time, you do get a shot at big money for minimal investment.

Big slot machine payoffs intrigue many people, and they are usually much better deals than state lotteries (although more and more frequently they use the same 20-year payout). Casinos in many states now offer interlinked machines with huge progressive jackpots, sometimes called "wide area progressives." One of the most famous of these is the Megabucks network.

Wide area progressives like Megabucks aren't run by one casino. A separate company produces and maintains the machines and the interstate computer network. The casinos just take a percentage of the action, but all of the administrative costs of advertising and running a multi-state network have to be paid for somehow, and, of course, the paying is ultimately done by the players.

Wide area progressives offer the same disadvantages of other Big Score play: The casino charges the player a premium for those dreams. The October 1997 *Las Vegas*

Advisor quoted the odds on hitting the new "Wheel of Fortune" progressive at 50 million to one. Even Duncan MacLeod wouldn't live long enough to hit it.

Smaller, individual progressive or small bank progressive machines offer more realistic possibilities. The wide-area progressive machines pay out much less hour to hour, because they need to hold something back for the really big payoff. On a less ambitious machine, you'll win small jackpots much more frequently and, for most people, that's a more fun way to play.

An even better approach is playing in a casino tournament. Casinos offer them in just about every game, even slots, and it's ideal Big Score gambling in that your potential loss usually (and preferably) is limited to the entry fee, while you can win a *lot* (how much is a function of the number of entrants—the more the merrier).

One of the most exciting and advantageous aspects of tournament gambling is that *someone has to win*. Although you are playing against the House, what really matters isn't so much your record against the House, as how well you did relative to the other players in the tournament. It is entirely possible that you could win a tournament with a net losing result at the tables, just because the other players lost more than you!

The only drawback to tournament play is that it usually leads only to a Sort of Big Score—thousands rather than millions. But to chase a few thousand at low risk, you can't beat a tournament, and the trophy remains long after the cash prize is spent.

Another good way to go for a Really Big Score is the old-fashioned way: letting your winnings ride at a game offering reasonable odds. For example, find a baccarat table with, say, a $20 minimum and $20,000 limit. Bet $20 on Player and let it ride...40...80...160...320...640 (starting to get awfully tempting to pull some of that back now, isn't it? Let's take $140 off the table—that'll give us seven more $20 chances to start a streak)...500...1,000...2,000...4,000...8,000....

Okay, now you *know* you're never going to bet $8,000, much less $16,000, so be honest and admit that when you make the $4,000 bet and win, you're going to stuff $4,000 into your pocket and just bet $4,000 again.

So you see the problem in the "let it ride" approach. Most of us just don't have the guts, or the stupidity, to make the huge bets needed to get to Big Score range. At some point on our personal Fear/Greed index, we decide that a few thousand is pretty darn good, and you know what? It is.

Just imagine how you would feel if you really let it ride without pulling back a nickel. 640...1,280...2,560...5,120...10,240...oops, sorry sir, very nice bet there. *Ten grand* down the hatch. Yikes. Personally, I like to start rat-holing (stuffing chips into my pockets) kind of early in the sequence, so I don't feel like a complete idiot when my luck runs out. Of course, if the streak goes on and on, you cost yourself money, but you're pretty happy anyway.

If you're really determined to let it ride, you can take yourself down to Binion's Horseshoe, a casino famous for its no-limit games. You can plunk down $5 on the craps table and try to hit 22 passes in a row, at which point you would have $10,485,760, less the cost of the new pants you would almost certainly have to buy.

For me, I think it would take a quart of Scotch to get me past 16 passes, when I had $163,840, but the odds on making it all the way to the $10,485,760 are less than 3 million to one, which beats the heck out of 18 million to one odds, a 20-year payout, and maybe having to share it in the lottery. Of course, there are important reasons why a quart of Scotch should not be part of a Big Score plan, and if you can't see them, please stay out of casinos.

So that's the trade-off in almost any form of going for The Big Score. If you let the state or the casino take the agony out of it, you get your Big Score without the chickening-out problem, but the house charges a *very* hefty odds premium for giving it to you all at once, making it much less likely that you will get your Big Score. If you have nerves of steel, you can try to run up a long winning streak, which will almost always mean either settling for a Sort of Big Score, or cursing yourself for going one bet further than you meant to.

Hey, I never said it was going to be easy. There's always the *really* old-fashioned way of making The Big Score— earning it.

Chapter 19

♥

How Much
Is the
Free Lunch Today?

As we all know, casinos are owned by nonprofit organizations that exist solely to provide an entertainment service to the public, and that donate all money won from gamblers to protect dolphins, whales, and rainforests.

What? They don't? I'm confused. I mean, they give players all those free drinks, and sometimes free food, rooms, or even airfare if they play enough. Why in the world would they do that unless they were public service-minded institutions?

Why indeed.

Even the most naive among us know why the drinks are free. Loosen the inhibitions and the purse-strings soon follow. Months of carefully managed results can burn up in just a few minutes of half-drunken plunging.

I hesitate to say anything about drinking, actually, because the best financial course is pretty obvious, and most players already know whether they like to drink when they play. Nonetheless, my conscience requires me to at least offer the advice, and then you can go right ahead and ignore it.

Consider this: Even if the casino *paid* you $5 for every free drink you accepted, you'd be making a bad deal. Casinos haven't tried this because it would make their position on drinking too obvious.

My concern isn't so much about a modest decline in your minute-to-minute playing abilities: If you find drinking fun, a slight decline in your skills and results might be an acceptable price to pay for the added fun.

The real danger is that you are far, far more vulnerable to a sudden meltdown of huge betting or tapping into heavy credit as you start drinking. I'd be much more comfortable if you drank when you were done playing for the night, and if your cash and credit cards were safely locked away somewhere. That keeps the potential for disaster to a minimum. End of lecture: Make your own choice.

What about other freebies (usually called "comps")? Can they be a good deal? If you're going to play anyway, why not accept all the goodies the casino is willing to give you? Remember that phrase: "If you're going to play *anyway.*" It's important.

There is an art to playing the comps game, and those who play it well can obtain more in the way of comps than someone else who gives the House equal (or even greater) action. There have been entire books written on this subject, and I teach a seminar about it, but I want to skip it for right now. There are more important lessons to learn first.

In the main, casinos don't give comps away to compete with other casinos (most competitive promotions take some other form). Casinos in the same town use similar formulae in determining to what comps your action entitles you.

Casinos give comps away for two reasons: First, and much more important, *to entice you to play longer or at a higher dollar level than you would without them.* Second, because it makes it easier for you to rationalize big losses (at least at some subconscious, rebellious level) and still return: "So what if I lost a bundle. They gave me a free room and treated me like a big shot."

For example, to earn an RFB (Room, Food, and Beverage) comp at a typical casino, you must average four hours of play a day while making $25 minimum bets. Averaging $25, instead of playing at a $25 minimum, is okay at some places. What does playing to try to meet this minimum mean to you?

It means that if you hit a losing streak, you can't call it quits for the day and take your shot tomorrow—instead, you keep playing while you're upset, and when you're more likely to do something foolish. It means you can't slow down to $5 bets when things aren't going your way. It means a hassle every time you want to switch tables.

And it especially means not leaving your base hotel to go play elsewhere. Two hours at Caesar's and two hours at the Hilton add up to four hours of play, but not a free room, because you gave neither hotel enough action.

Heck, they might as well quit fencing and just clamp a chain around your ankle.

The single most powerful weapon you have in your battle with the casino is your own free will: your right to play sensibly, to stop when you're tired, to play only as often as you want, when and where you want. Playing more just to try to earn casino comps is the gaming equivalent, if you'll pardon a biblical analogy, of selling your birthright for a mess of pottage.

If you're going to play anyway, accepting comps makes a lot of sense, especially for slot players, who tend to stay in one place (often at one machine), and who are playing a game that by its very nature doesn't allow for sudden plunges—you can't shove 500 coins into a slot machine in a desperate attempt to get even quickly.

Slot comps are also easy to manage, since you get rated by putting a card in the machine, instead of having to get a floorperson's attention, and your points accrue over time, so (at least in some clubs) you can earn something over the course of several trips even if you don't manage it in one. So make sure you join one or more slot clubs, take the time to compare what the different clubs offer you for your play, and consider giving most or all of your action to the casino with the best club.

Comps for table games don't accumulate like slot club points; they're strictly a "what have you done for me lately" proposition. This makes a big difference in my attitude about them, relative to slot clubs, and hopefully in yours too.

For table game players, if you can make not one single bet more than you would have otherwise, and can pick yourself up and leave if the vibe isn't right...then go ahead and get rated and ask for as much as possible. All they can do is say no (actually, they'll probably say, "you need to play another hour making bigger bets," and there you have the reason they offer comps).

In 29 years of playing and people-watching in casinos, I have observed *very* few people who have enough self-discipline to play the comps game. In the heat of the moment, most people can find some kind of rationalization for betting more or playing longer even *without* the promise of comps, and adding it can crumble the best of intentions. The whole deal is very seductive, by design.

If you're old enough to remember the TV Western farce *F-Troop*, you might remember the running gag about the daily price of the town Saloon's free lunch. "How much is the free lunch today?" Corporal Agarn would ask. And he would get a straight answer, usually different, and never free.

So remember the acronym TANSTAAFL: There Ain't No Such Thing As A Free Lunch. If a casino is willing to give you something, it's because they know that they're getting something better in return. Your freedom of choice is worth a lot. Don't sell it cheaply.

Chapter 20

♠

Are You a TEF Guy?

A lot of people think that "sensible gambling" is an oxymoron—you know, one of those internally inconsistent phrases like "jumbo shrimp," "death benefits," or "legal ethics."

Although it's certainly true that gambling leads to trouble or even financial ruin for some people, it's equally true that a person who understands *both* the game he or she is playing *and* his or her own nature can lose sums small enough to justify gambling as a pleasant diversion, and even win occasionally.

The best things in life may well be free, but a lot of fun activities cost money: sporting events, live music, fine dining, movies, scuba diving, whatever. Unless you're very poor or very rich, you probably spend a good-sized percentage of your paycheck on fun.

No one condemns this, unless you're spending the kids' tuition money on trips to Hawaii. As long as what you spend on fun doesn't cut into necessities, you're on solid ground.

Gambling certainly can be fun, but it gets a bad rap—in many cases deserved—because people often lose more than they can afford, and more than an "entertainment budget" would allow.

Put another way, the cost of a scuba trip is much easier to calculate than the cost of a gambling trip, because short-run gambling results are unpredictable. You can play the same game, in the same casino, for the same length of time, using the same betting patterns for seven days running and have wildly different results each day.

In the long run, gambling results become more predictable, and with experience you will learn how to predict those results. Regardless of where you are on the learning curve, though, I urge you to follow what I call The Entertainment Formula, or TEF.

To use TEF, stop and consider the various ways you spend money on fun (not what your friends or relatives spend, but *you*. TEF is a very individual formula). Write down how much you spend for an evening at the movies, going to a baseball game, taking a ski trip, whatever it is that you do for fun. Then look for a pattern, a comfort level you have in your entertainment spending. Credit card and checking statements will help.

For most people, entertainment spending varies. Maybe three times a month you have a $60 night out. Maybe once a month you have a $200 night out or a $600 weekend. Maybe twice a year you take a $2,000 vacation. Maybe your numbers are 10 times that size, or maybe they're much smaller—plug in whatever numbers work. Be liberal in your definition of entertainment.

Eventually you will see your pattern in entertainment spending, and then you can start to look at substituting gambling for these other activities.

Suppose your pattern involves taking periodic mini-vacations that cost about $600. Perhaps a weekend in Las

Vegas would cost you $300, exclusive of gambling. Pretty clearly, a $300 gambling budget for that trip starts to suggest itself, because you would spend the same $600 total.

It's not quite that simple, because you're comparing apples and oranges. How much fun is the gambling trip, compared with what you do on the $600 mini-vacation? Maybe you find gambling a lot more fun...so maybe it's worth going higher on the gambling budget. Maybe gambling is a lot more fun if you win, but much less fun, maybe even miserable, if you lose.

If the gambling trip is always a lot more fun than your $600 weekend, then it's starting to look like going gambling makes sense for you. But if a little is good, is more better? That is, does it make sense to increase your gambling budget?

The answer depends not only on your total entertainment budget, but also on what you're going to do with the extra money—increase the size of your bets, or play more hours.

Only you can know what kind of thrill you like best— maybe bigger bets do it for you. Most people, though, have more fun playing two hours at $5 a hand than one hour at $10 a hand, or playing four hours on a quarter slot rather than one hour on a dollar slot, and the expected results are about the same.

They're not *exactly* the same—dollar slots usually pay back a slightly higher percentage—but they are close enough for this analysis.

Here's an even bigger issue: Suppose you know yourself well enough to know that if you gamble and win $300, you feel pretty good—not ecstatic, but pleased. You also know that if you lose $300, you're downright miserable. In other words, you hate losing more than you enjoy winning. If that's so, consider finding another hobby, because it's likely that losing trips are going to occur more often than winning ones.

If, on the other hand, the reverse is true—you can shrug off a loss without much pain but simply glow when you win—gambling becomes a sensible way to spend your entertainment dollar.

So although it isn't possible to reduce your gambling decision to a cold equation, you can get close. As long as you are honest with yourself about your gambling results—both the dollar amounts and how those results make you feel—you can make an intelligent decision about whether gambling offers enough bang for your entertainment buck.

A lot of gamblers lie to their friends about their results, and I won't editorialize about that here. But you must be honest with yourself, or you're asking for trouble.

Of course, if you don't view gambling as entertainment, but rather as a good chance to improve your personal balance sheet, buy a new car, or upgrade your lifestyle, please give me a call at 1-888-ODDS-WIN. I have a couple of much better investments for you. One of them is this bridge in Brooklyn, and the other is an incredible deal on some swampland in Florida.

Chapter 21

♣

The Only
Game
in Town

People who want to gamble in casinos have a lot more options today than they did 20 years ago. Las Vegas and Atlantic City have grown mightily, and the riverboat and Indian casinos have brought the games much closer to home. So where does it make the most sense to play?

Increased competition almost always means a better deal for consumers, in both the retail and service industries. Whenever you can go somewhere else, a business either provides you with good service at a reasonable price or risks losing you to the competition.

The gaming world is no different, as anyone who braved the long lines when Resorts was the only Atlantic City casino can attest. Resorts had a monopoly and they knew it, so they could make their tables $25 minimum, and if you didn't like it, you could always fly to Las Vegas.

These days, competition in Atlantic City is almost as keen as it is in Las Vegas, which means not only can you find the right game at the right price, but also that they have to treat you well. If you have a reasonable complaint, they will usually treat it fairly and respectfully. There are competitive promotions, good deals in restaurants, and all the little things that help you decide to stay at Casino A instead of Casino B.

So scout around a little when you go to Las Vegas or Atlantic City. You might want to pay particular attention to the casinos that have to compete in less than ideal locations. Off-strip casinos like the Rio have to do something to make up for the inconvenience, and they do it in lots of little ways.

The big difference, though, comes when you visit a casino that doesn't have any local competition. Although in a sense all casinos have competition because you can indeed get on a plane and go to Las Vegas (or pick a different form of entertainment entirely), if a casino does not have any local competitors, and if it is run by people who are either greedy or stupid, you might find yourself at a big disadvantage.

I first became aware of this phenomenon playing poker in Texas, in an Indian casino located more than 200 miles from the nearest casino. Two players in my game engaged in conduct that was either incredibly stupid, or cheating via partnership play.

When I told the poker room manager what had happened, his response was not "I'm sorry, Sir, I'll check it out," or "I know the players in question, Sir, and I think it very unlikely they were cheating," but the considerably less accommodating "There are no partnerships at the X Casino, Sir." And he turned on his heel and walked away.

In other words, he didn't give a damn about what I thought or about appeasing me. He had a captive audience in the only legal poker place around, and he knew it. Putting the best possible face on it, maybe he was just supporting the locals. Fortunately, I was "just passing through," as they used to say in that part of Texas, and so I wasn't faced with a decision about returning.

Please understand: If any cheating was going on, it was *not* by the house. Casinos make their poker money either by raking a percentage of each pot or by charging an hourly fee; as a result, there is no motivation to cheat. If anything funny was happening, my fellow players were behind it.

As I moseyed (one of two ways to walk in Texas, I'm told) out of the poker room into the main casino, I surveyed the variation of blackjack played there. It was similar to classic blackjack, but just different enough so that my basic strategy table would need refining unless I was willing to play at some unknown disadvantage. I wasn't.

Next I ambled past the slot machine area, and started wondering just what, if any, Casino Commission was monitoring slot payoffs. After all, it's neither immoral nor illegal to run tough games. Did the casino have any statistics about slot payoff percentages? No one was talking that night. Perhaps they'd have told me if I wrote to them. The information certainly wasn't available easily.

My poker experience notwithstanding, I was quite sure no cheating was going on in the slot or blackjack areas, for the same reason virtually no cheating goes on in Las Vegas: The casino's built-in edge is good enough to provide the owners with a very nice legitimate way to take your money. Why risk everything to take it more quickly? If you lose too fast, you won't come back.

Just because the games were honest doesn't mean they were a good deal, though. Just as the convenience store on the corner charges more for milk than the big supermarket, this casino was almost certainly "charging" (milking?) its customers a higher house percentage than a Las Vegas casino would, because it was more convenient for the locals to drive there than to fly somewhere and stay in a hotel.

Now, I shop in convenience stores from time to time, because on some occasions I'm willing to pay a little more for the convenience. But I'm doing it with my eyes open. I know I'm paying more, and I know exactly how much more.

When you play in an out-of-the-way casino, there's a good chance you're going to pay something extra, whether it comes in the form of a higher house percentage, or less customer service. Maybe that something extra is worth it, if you like gambling, and your alternative is the cost of a plane ticket to Vegas and a hotel room. And perhaps if you are a recognized local, you might get a better brand of customer service.

But me, I think I'll stick to towns that have local competition, or to the gaming supercities of Las Vegas, Reno/Tahoe or Atlantic City, where they not only offer highly competitive games, but also offer all sorts of fun non-gambling entertainment: shows, theme parks, virtual reality rides, that sort of thing. And the next time I'm in that part of Texas, I'll just pass on through, sheriff.

Chapter 22

◆

Easy Come,
Easy Go?
NO, NO, NO!

Now here's a tough problem: What do you do when you win a whole lot of money?

Most readers will retort that on the grand scale of important gambling problems, "What I do with a big win" belongs near the bottom. Too much money, after all, usually doesn't create the kind of problems that too little causes.

That's a dangerous attitude. One of the reasons players expose themselves to the risk of losing big is the corresponding chance of winning big, and winning big most certainly does happen. But if you don't handle that big win carefully, you'll go broke almost as fast as someone who never wins, maybe faster!

Suppose, for example, you go to Las Vegas once a month, and you lose $5,000 each time during your January, March, May, July, September, and November trips, but win $5,000 each time during your February, April, June, August, October, and December trips. In other words, you alternate winning and losing $5,000 per trip throughout the year.

Come December 31, when you total your results for the year, you find that you've broken exactly even. Not a bad result at all, especially since you had so much fun while gambling.

Now let's add a little dose of danger to this hypothetical gaming year. Let's suppose that you celebrated each of those big wins with a wild spending spree: champagne, caviar, fancy restaurants, big tipping, expensive presents, maybe risky investments or loans to friends with spotty repayment records. In short, all the usual suspects and indicia of money burning a hole in your pocket.

Well, perhaps those spending sprees are fun, but let's say that each one costs you $2,000, and that you never would have spent the money, except that you felt rich each time, and an easy-come, easy-go attitude created your indulgence.

Now when you assess the year on December 31, you haven't broken even. You're down $12,000 (although perhaps up a few pounds from all that good eating). Your gambling was a break-even proposition, but because you treated money *won* with less respect than money *earned*, you wound up a loser.

That's just one scenario; there are others. Suppose the first few months of the year are the winning months and you go up $20,000. Flush with all that cash, you go buy a new car, or take on some other kind of long-term expense. Now your luck changes, and you lose $30,000 over the next few months.

In this scenario, you're not only down a net $10,000 on your gambling, but you've also taken on long-term expenses, like that car payment, which put pressure on you, perhaps enough pressure so that you're no longer comfortable gambling. Now you've lost $10,000, are driving a too-expensive car, *and* you can't afford your favorite hobby.

One final variation of the spending spree problem, before we look at how you can protect your successes: Suppose you win a bundle on the first day of your casino trip, and you have three days to go before you leave. This is a dangerous variation, because Vegas is full of ways that a winner can blow cash in a hurry.

Although there are many different kinds of expensive goods and services available in Las Vegas, the easiest and most common way to blow those winnings is with more gambling. Big winners tend to make less discriminating bets than players up or down a little. A solid craps player starts betting all the Hardways. A blackjack-only player starts experimenting with Caribbean Stud. A $1 slot player decides to try the roulette tables. It happens.

If you make enough bad bets, you can give it all back in a big hurry. Don't think a good gambler wouldn't act that way. I've seen good gamblers win big money in a blackjack tournament, take their winnings directly to a craps table, and halve them in 15 minutes. The "rush" from a big win can be more intoxicating than alcohol, with the same impact on judgment.

Sure, those good gamblers might have kept winning, but they made the money with smart bets and gave it back with silly bets. Smart bets win more often. What can you do to protect yourself from this easy-come, easy-go problem?

If you're still in Las Vegas, take a break from gambling for at least the rest of the day or evening, so that some of the rush wears off.

Although this requires a bit of discipline it is a heck of a lot more fun than most kinds of self-discipline, because you're walking around town like you own it, sneering at all the pathetic losers, feeling superior to everyone in sight, enjoying your riches merely by possessing them. What's wrong with feeling like a winner for a while?

It's unrealistic, and probably not much fun, to plan no more gambling for two or three days. Instead, figure out a way to secure a good portion of your winnings, even if you have to go to Western Union and wire some money to someone who'll hold it for you.

Once you're sure of bringing most of it home, you can have some fun playing the way you normally do. If that level of action doesn't thrill your newly rich self, pick yourself up and leave. Vegas will still be there next month, when you can start with a more realistic attitude.

If your big win happens near the end of your trip, and you merely have to protect yourself from going crazy when you're home, figure out how many days or weeks you would have to work to earn that much, consider how hard you would have to work for that money, and then ask yourself if you really want to blow it in a hurry.

Next, remember that your chances of losing a big sum next time are probably much better than your chances of duplicating your big win. If you can put the big win away for the inevitable rainy losing day, you'll be able to absorb the loss without changing your lifestyle, or suddenly ruling out an expensive college for your children.

The simplest one-sentence rule: *Easy come, easy go is for suckers*. Just because the money came to you easily doesn't mean you have to throw it away. You might need it someday when the dice aren't rolling so well for you, or when you want to spend it on something important. Most gamblers visit "tap city" (go broke) *not* because they lose every dime gambling, but rather because they're careless with money when they win and so don't have a reserve when they lose.

I'm not saying that you can't ever celebrate a big win; I'm all in favor of treating yourself well. Just postpone the celebration long enough so that a bit of judgment returns.

You'll keep your money, to say nothing of your self-respect, a whole lot longer.

Another variation of the easy-come, easy-go problem occurs when you've come into a large sum of money *before* you ever get to Las Vegas. Maybe you inherited a lot of money, or just got your Christmas bonus, sold your house, or whatever. The newly rich tend to treat money with less respect than they should, especially in the first days, weeks, or months after acquiring it.

Remember the "nest egg" in Albert Brooks' movie, *Lost in America*? Albert and his wife decided to sell everything, buy a mobile home, and drop out of Corporate America. Full of both romance and cash, they decided to stop in Las Vegas, not to gamble but to renew their wedding vows. They lost their nest egg—their life savings—the first night there.

Few people are likely to repeat the "nest egg" fiasco in its fullest extreme, but it's human nature to want to cut loose after a lifetime of being careful. If your money is burning a hole in your pocket when you get to Las Vegas, the likelihood is that it will eventually burn all the way through.

In sum, although Las Vegas is certainly a fun place to hang out when you're dripping with cash, that's precisely when the danger to your bankroll is at its highest, and your ability to think clearly and protect your bankroll is at its lowest. Why risk a moment of weakness that you'll regret the rest of your life? Do yourself a favor and consider going somewhere else right after you get rich. Vegas will still be there in a month or two, when your equilibrium has returned...and so will your cash.

Chapter 23

♥

The Champion's Choice: Intuition or Logic?

For most of my gambling career, if you'd asked me to define the role that intuition plays in gambling, I'd have said something like, "Intuition is an important part of gambling, if you like losing."

These days, I'm not quite so sure.

Don't get me wrong. For the most part, mathematical and logical gamblers are winners, and intuitive gamblers are losers. The rules involving odds are called the "laws" of probability for a reason, and it's not so you can ignore them like the speed limit.

Anyone who tries to gamble without a solid grounding in the probabilities of his or her game of choice, or who plays in a casino without any notion of the house percentages, or who routinely ignores conventional wisdom about the best way to play a game like blackjack, will lose, and probably lose quickly.

Indeed, the main reason why I scoffed at intuition for so long is that I always saw it used as an excuse for poor, impulsive, or just plain silly play. I'd be playing blackjack and someone at the table would hit a hard 16 with a dealer

4 showing (a really awful play), and they'd say, "I have a feeling about it."

My experience is that such feelings are right five times out of 13 (because five cards—the Ace, 2, 3, 4, or 5—will help the hand and the other eight—6, 7, 8, 9, 10, J, Q, or K—will bust it), and, of course, even those five good cards don't guarantee victory, but merely a chance to fight the dealer's own hand.

At the poker table, where most players are looking for any possible excuse to play a hand instead of folding, intuition really gets a bad name (although it's an important part of expert-level poker). The words "I've got a feeling" often precede a bad decision to call a bet from an obviously better hand.

Indeed, for a long time I viewed the logical approach taken by *Star Trek's* Mr. Spock as the ideal way to gamble, and even today I feel it far superior to the way most gamblers play. But then I saw *Star Trek VI, The Undiscovered Country*, where, lo and behold, Spock told his pupil, "Logic is the beginning of understanding, not its end."

Good enough for Spock, good enough for me. Not long after seeing *Trek VI* (just a coincidence, I promise) I spent some time looking into my own previously undiscovered country—feelings, intuition, matters that cannot yet be explained by science and logic—and emerged far less convinced that I understand everything about how the world works.

One of the key moments in that quest was a Laura Day seminar on intuition. Laura, whose books *Practical Intuition* and *Practical Intuition for Success* are bestsellers, has something going for her that logic can't touch, and I'd advise you to look at her writing even if you were going to ignore its potential for impact on your gambling.

More to the point, I emerged from my study believing that *if* one starts with logic, and uses logic and math as the *beginning* of gambling understanding, then (and *only* then) the softer sciences can expand your gaming bag of tricks.

Does that mean I advocate following your feelings when you're faced with a hard 16 and the dealer has a 4 showing? No. Maybe Laura and a few other people out there have that kind of intuition, but until Laura or one of her students like Lissy Jones signs off on your potential, using your intuition to discard your logic is only asking for trouble.

I most definitely do not advocate using intuition and feelings as a *substitute* for study and technically accurate play. Instead, I believe it can be a helpful *supplement* to technical accuracy, because there are many situations where logic and math provide no help.

What kind of situations? I'm okay with using intuition for picking the right blackjack table, making a decision in the complete absence of data, or deciding when to leave a casino. I think we all take in a lot of information at a sub-conscious level, and where our science fails us, our subconscious may be able to help.

In other words, using intuition can be a way to apply data you've picked up, without even realizing it. When I'm playing poker trying to decide whether to call an opponent's bet, I'm analyzing first. How did the opponent bet the hand earlier? What cards have I seen (or not seen) that would help his hand? Is he winning, or losing, and what impact does that have on his betting? How does his play this hand compare with what he's done in others? Is he a strong player? And these questions only *begin* the analysis.

Nonetheless, after I've run through all the analysis, I often still don't have a clear answer. Then, and only then, I'm willing to go with a feeling. It may be that I have sub-consciously noticed something about my opponent's body language, it may be something I'm unable to understand, or it may be nonsense. But once I've exhausted my logic, I'm willing to look for more.

What does all of this mean for you, on your next casino trip? Not much. Most of my readers are not advanced enough in their studies of gambling to start breaking rules, and until you have a solid foundation of technically correct play, intuition isn't much help.

So don't halt your study of that basic strategy black-jack chart. *Please* do not use my endorsement of intuition as "potentially useful in some situations" as a license to do whatever you want whenever you want. Gambling that way is what gets people into trouble, and if your intuition were any good, you'd know that!

Instead, be willing to trust your feelings about matters you can't look up in a book. The right time to quit, to change seats, to take a break—I'm all in favor of following feelings that tell you to stop gambling for a little while. Usually these impulses are very helpful.

But if your "feelings" tell you to get out of bed at 2:30 a.m. and go bet $500 on the pass line, turn over and go back to sleep. *That's not intuition.* That's your desire to gamble looking for an excuse to indulge itself, and if there's one area where my intuition and my lengthy study of gambling always agree, this is it.

Similarly, if your intuition tells you to keep playing when you're losing badly, because you "have a feeling" things are going to turn around, quit using your intuition in gambling situations. *You're just looking for an excuse to keep playing.* And although you'll probably find an excuse if you want one badly enough, I don't want any part of it.

If you're disciplined enough to make all the technically correct plays, and use your intuition for matters beyond the technical, you'll live long and prosper. I have a strong feeling that it's the logical thing to do.

PART FIVE:

Advice for Specific Games and Situations

Chapter 24

♠

OnE-ArmEd Bandits and Their Two-Legged Customers

I first became aware of the nearly hypnotic hold that slot machines have on their players when my family took a trip to Las Vegas when I was 13. After a few hours we were supposed to go to dinner, and I very nearly had to carry my grandmother out of the casino. "Go away!" she said with a vehemence I'd never heard from her before. "This machine is going to hit soon, I know it!"

Eventually my mother convinced Grandma to take a break, but I knew then and there that I never wanted to be in thrall to a machine like Grandma was. Of course, if you took my Macintosh computer away I would start crying, but that's different somehow, I'm sure.

I've never entered "slot hypnosis" quite like Grandma, but I've been lured into slot territory from time to time, and have picked up some tidbits of slot wisdom to pass along.

First, make sure you understand what kind of machine you're playing. On some machines, playing two or three coins merely doubles or triples payoffs, so there's no real need to play multiple coins. On most machines, though, playing anything less than maximum coins is a recipe for disaster. The jackpot can come up and you won't win it!

Once while in the Bahamas I started talking to an attractive young woman playing a dollar machine, and while I usually avoid giving advice to strangers (if the advice works they don't know you, and if it doesn't they're furious), this woman seemed so nice I wanted to help out.

"You know that machine you're playing won't pay the $1,000 jackpot if you hit, because you're only playing one dollar," I said. "You have to play three dollars to win."

"Oh, well I guess I better play three, then," she said, "but I don't think my money will last very long that way, I only have 20 dollars." She dropped three dollars into the slot, pulled the handle, and hit the jackpot! She was thrilled, as (sigh) no doubt was the boyfriend she was returning to Canada to see the next day. Ah, well, you know what they say, lucky at cards, unlucky at love.

On the same issue, make sure, before you pull the handle, that all lights or lines are lit. Sometimes coins drop straight through to the tray and you're only playing two coins when you think you've played three. Believe me, the casino won't believe you. If the machine hits a three-coin jackpot and it says you only played two, you're out of luck.

All machines list their jackpots, but it's important to note if the jackpot is a number of coins, or dollars—it makes a difference. 10,000 nickels is only $500, so if you dump roll after roll of nickels into a machine hoping for the big payoff, you might be disappointed.

Sooner or later you will have to make a decision: Do you want to play high progressive jackpot machines that offer great dreaming possibilities but fewer and smaller steady payoffs, or less ambitious machines like the one my friend hit in the Bahamas, where the jackpot is not enormous, but the chances of hitting it are more realistic?

Progressive slots come in three main types—the wide area progressives like Megabucks, smaller progressive banks of perhaps eight or 12 machines arranged in an oval, and individual progressive machines.

If you play a small bank or individual machine, you can help your cause by searching out machines that have not been hit recently. I've seen players on a machine just reset to the minimum $250 jackpot, with an identical machine offering a $3,000 jackpot available four feet away. I suppose the theory was, "This machine paid off once, it will again," but a smart player will look for the maximum jackpot.

It's harder than you think to hit the big progressive jackpots. On old-style machines, three reels of 20 stops meant a maximum 8,000 combinations (20x20x20=8,000). These days the reels *look* like they have the same 20 stops, but actually the number of stops is controlled by computer, up to 256 stops per reel, and 256x256x256 equals—are you ready?—*16,777,216* possible combinations. Gee, no wonder you didn't hit the jackpot before lunch.

If that isn't enough to give you pause, on a four-reel machine there can be as many as 4,294,967,296 possibilities (256x256x256x256). So even though those Megabucks or Quartermania jackpots seem by casual inspection easy enough to hit, they're not.

I think a good way to play (assuming you're going to play slots in the first place) is to spend most of your time at less ambitious machines, receiving more frequent payoffs, and just to dabble a bit with the big jackpot machines, to feed your dreams of The Big Score.

Because slot machines are *the* most popular casino game, and because—despite what many people think—there are critically important things to know about playing slots, we're going to linger in the slot zone a while longer. In the next two chapters, you'll learn what some of the world's sharpest slot players do to improve their odds.

Chapter 25

♣

Video Poker and Other Smart Slot Machine Plays

One reason why slots are so popular is that, barring a miscalculation on the number of coins to play, there isn't much pressure to make a good decision, like in poker or blackjack, and the layout isn't intimidating, as it can be at craps or roulette. But there's a compromise that offers some of the best of both worlds: the video poker slot.

Video poker slots are reasonably easy to play—most people can learn to play fairly well in perhaps one to three hours of study—and I think they offer more satisfaction when you win, since it feels like your decision to draw one or two cards had something to do with your win.

Another very good reason to favor video poker slots is that they often pay back higher percentages than the average slot machine. One perverse way to verify this is to see how most slot clubs don't give you as much credit for playing video poker as for playing the other slots. Be warned, though: Video poker slots are also the most addicting form of gambling around, so if you have tendencies in that area, be careful.

One other important video poker note: While you can learn to play "fairly well" in a few hours, there will be a big difference in the results of someone playing fairly well and someone playing perfectly. So if you're planning on spending a lot of time playing video poker, you'll want to spend a lot more time in study and practice than the occasional recreational player.

Another major slot decision is what kind of machine to play: nickel, quarter, half-dollar, dollar, or higher ($5 slots are becoming more common and you can find $500 slots at some big hotels).

The higher denomination machines (dollar instead of nickel, for example) usually pay better return *percentages*, but this is *far* less important than the money-management principle of playing the size machine appropriate to your budget. Playing max coins on a dollar slot, you can lose a lot of cash in a very short time.

What about my grandmother's theory (Chapter 24) that her machine was ready to hit? I've never understood this one. If a baseball player strikes out four times in a row, most fans hope that someone else will come up to bat in the bottom of the ninth. In almost every other form of gambling, players expect that both good and bad streaks will continue, but when slots are involved, many people seem to think differently.

There are a lot of technical slot machine manufacturing reasons why the "ready to hit" theory is wrong, most of which involve the constantly moving microprocessor-controlled random number generators (RNGs) inside the slots. I'll spare you the scientific details, but believe me, a cold machine is no more likely to hit than any other machine, and it could be cold simply because the casino has set it at a lower percentage than others in the area.

So if a machine is unkind to you, don't throw good money after bad. Go find a different one. And while you're at it, make sure you're playing in a pleasant atmosphere. The smoker next to you bothering you? Move somewhere else. Is some annoying know-it-all offering you tips about playing max coins? Well, come to think of it maybe that's okay.

A lot of slot players are hesitant to move, because they are afraid to leave a machine and then have someone else hit it immediately, but the random number generators mean you don't have to agonize about this. The random numbers are changing every millisecond, and if you had stayed one pull longer you certainly would have pulled the handle at a different millisecond than the next player. So at least intellectually you can know you did not pull out too soon. Emotionally, it is harder to accept or believe this.

For example, the existence of RNGs complicates my story about my Canadian friend's $1,000 jackpot (Chapter 24). True, she would not have won the jackpot without following my advice about three coins. But the jackpot was not "destined" to come up on her next pull. My interruption of her play changed the split-second at which she pulled the handle. If she had pulled even a hundredth of a second earlier or later, some other sequence would have shown up. So my interruption for advice was still fortuitous...but it actually didn't save her from a horror story. In all likelihood, she just would have had some other non-jackpot combination show up.

So when someone hits a jackpot on a machine you've just finished playing, there's no need for anger, despair, or any other negative emotions. Go with "envy" if you simply have to feel something negative. But because most people don't take vacations in order to wallow around in negative emotions, you'll be happier if you just enjoy the new person's success for them.

Now, if you're playing a progressive slot, either one of the wide-area progressives, or even just one tied to a relatively small bank of slots, and someone next to you hits *that* jackpot, then you have at least a tiny legitimate right to feel some regret...because you will certainly need to get up and move to a different machine. It's never worth playing a progressive machine right after it hits, because the progressive resets to a relatively low amount.

A buddy of mine got to observe this in action one time, playing one of a dozen connected video poker machines. He was sitting next to this very nice-looking and pleasant woman who was, by his estimate, "at least 90 years old and probably older." My friend hit the jackpot, and the women turned to him and said with a face that could have turned a lesser man to stone, "You fu - - er." Yessir, gambling brings out the best in many of us.

Let's get back to moving around and what that really means. For one, it can mean more than just moving from one machine to another. You may want to move to a different kind of machine, or even to another casino, if you're not doing well where you are, especially if the new casino advertises high (greater than 97 percent) rates of return.

Even if you're in such a casino, it's important to remember that all machines are most definitely *not* created equal. Some machines will be set to pay off at better percentages than others. A few concepts to remember:

* Slots very close to table games are often set lower, because losing table players sometimes wander over to slots on a break, and the casino would prefer that they return to their losing table game ways, where they will lose faster.

* Slots lined up near buffet lines are often set lower, because the casino has a captive audience that won't be staying in one place very long.

* Slots in entrances to slot areas, or in other high-traffic areas (but not next to the table games) are often set higher, because the casinos figure that as long as someone has to hit a jackpot now and then, they might as well do it someplace where a lot of people will see it (it's advertising that draws in other players).

* Pick not only your machine, but also your seat with care. An end seat means you've cut in half your risk of an obnoxious person or heavy smoker sitting next to you! On the other hand, if increased social interaction is one of your goals, then an end seat is not as desirable.

* Playing two or more machines simultaneously increases your risk in a number of ways. First, you're playing faster, which generally means you're losing faster. Second, it makes you far more vulnerable to thieves who look to steal money from unwatched trays. Third, it makes you more vulnerable to making a mistake, such as pulling a handle when only two of the three coins have registered. And, finally, because casinos know that people often play two machines simultaneously, they are unlikely to put two good machines right next to each other. That way, any "double" player is guaranteed to be playing at least one bad machine.

* For those of you looking for every possible edge, pick a desirable seat with a view toward selling it to someone else. A seat next to a beautiful woman or a handsome man might be worth something to someone, just as a seat at a hot machine might be. You might be able to get $10 or $20 from the right person. Some players try to ask for a percentage of winnings in return for giving up a seat, but that strikes

me both as a bit greedy, and a deal not likely to be honored. Personally, I think "seat-selling" takes unfair advantage of human superstition, and so I neither do it nor recommend it, but I have known players down on their luck who have made a few dollars this way.

* Make sure you collect when you win, and when you leave! Sometimes a machine won't have enough coins in the hopper to pay off a jackpot, and a small, "see attendant" light will flash. If you put another coin in and resume play before you get paid, you're out of luck. Similarly, most machines now have a button you can push to get paid in coin for any credits you have left over. Remember to push it before you rush off to lunch, and make sure you're paid what you're due! If the machine runs out of money (which can happen easily), you need an attendant either to pay you off or to refill the machine. If you need an attendant, *do not* wander away from your machine to find one, or someone else might try to claim your money! Although casino surveillance cameras make an interloper's success unlikely, it isn't impossible.

Finally, remember that slots share one important trait with all other casino games: House percentages grind away at your bankroll. If you pull the handle 300 times an hour (not at all difficult: pros can hit 600 per hour!), your money will last only half as long as someone who pulls a more leisurely 150 times an hour. That's a big advantage to slot play: Unlike blackjack, craps, or roulette, *you* determine the betting pace, not the dealer. The casino offers you few enough chances to take control. Why not take advantage of one when they do?

Chapter 26

◆

It's Not Polite to Point at a Slot Machine... Unless It's With Your Pinky

A slot pro friend of mine who wishes to be known as "Pinky" for purposes of this book (because he is busy making money from casinos and doesn't want any more visibility than he "enjoys" already), offers some telling advice for casual slot players.

Pinky (who makes a *very* good living playing slots) says: "My tip for slots is to read 98-percent payout billboards as 'we will take 2 percent of your money compounded every six seconds if you are sucker enough to sit here.'"

Wow. Let's look at what Pinky's statement implies.

First, some quick math with Pinky's "compounded every six seconds" line indicates he is indeed playing at a rate of 600 pulls per hour. Yet he calls the regular players "suckers" (a term I think too strong and too negative for most recreational players) for playing at high speed, so by implication, he's saying SLOW DOWN if you're a recreational player, and he's right.

"Hold the phone," you say. "That doesn't make sense. Pinky is making a very good living playing slots, and he plays fast. Why shouldn't I?"

You shouldn't because there is something very different about how Pinky plays and how he sees others play...and you'll see what when you read his next tip:

"Only play progressive slots at top coin, and spend a long time doing research by counting the mean time between jackpots and the average 'drop'."

We talked about this one for a while, because it's a bit more complicated than it seems. Pinky plays video poker slots almost exclusively (he won't say which ones and I don't blame him one bit), and because he does it for a living and not for recreation, time he spends observing slots is part of his business.

The "drop" to which he refers is the amount of money literally dropped into a given slot machine over time (see the Glossary for more about this). There isn't any easy way for players to figure out the casino's expected percentage win of the drop at most games (and it's hardly the kind of information they would put out front on the marquee), but patient players can learn a little about slot drops simply by watching one or more machines.

Although standing around watching other people play isn't most players' idea of fun, it is an inexpensive way to learn which machines are set to pay out at higher rates of return, especially if you plan on playing for a long time, at high rates of speed, or at higher denomination slots. It's not always obvious and you can't assume that identical-looking machines are set the same way. Indeed, Pinky relates a story where he observed two banks of identical-looking slots that were tied in electronically to the very same progressive slot jackpot, and where his observations proved over time that one bank of machines was set to return 85 percent and the identical bank right next to it 95 percent!

In Pinky's game of choice, video poker, an expert wins in the long run by playing correct basic video poker strategy (the subject of another book), and by playing machines whose progressive jackpots have built up to a point where the payoff for the big jackpot (awarded when the player hits a royal flush) offers better odds than the chances of hitting the big jackpot.

Another reason why players like Pinky can expect to win in the long run is that their optimal strategy is more complicated than the basic strategy most players employ, a complication analogous to the way that blackjack card counters alter blackjack basic strategy based on a card count.

Pinky, for example, explained that his optimum strategy involves "break points," where the plays change depending on the size of the jackpot. With 66JQX (poker shorthand for a pair of sixes, a Jack, a Queen, and any other random card) you usually keep the pair at normal jackpots, but might discard the pair if the Jack and Queen were suited, if the royal flush progressive payoff were extremely high. To make such decisions perfectly, you must know, "How high is high?" and this takes computer simulations or other calculations.

Another difference between Pinky's play and yours is that he can make 600 decisions an hour for hours on end without making an error. Even if you're making only 150 decisions an hour, you're probably not going to play error-free. And the difference between being a 101-percent return long-term favorite and a 99-percent long-term underdog doesn't require many errors.

So in video poker, just as in blackjack, baseball, golf, and indeed almost every kind of gambling game or sport, the way the professionals play is very different from the way most of us play, and to expect results similar to a professional without the professional's training and talent is about the same as a weekend hacker expecting to beat Tiger Woods in a round of golf. It just isn't going to happen.

As Pinky's Jack-Queen suited example shows, professional video poker strategy is based primarily around the chances of hitting a royal flush, and how much it will pay when it does hit.

As a result, most video poker pros have many more losing sessions than winning sessions. Lose, lose, lose, lose, lose, lose, lose and then, *Boom!,* hit a royal flush, which more than makes up for the losing sessions. Not everyone is cut out for that kind of approach, especially not recreational players who might only be dabbling for a few hours.

Although a recreational player certainly might hit a royal flush in such a short time, it's far more likely than a lot of money will go into the machine and not much will come out. So if you're just looking for a few hours of entertainment, a nice non-progressive machine might be more fun.

Chapter 27

♥

The Gambler's Ultimate Weapon

In Douglas Adams' *Hitchhiker's Guide to the Galaxy* series, a warlike alien civilization instructs its most powerful computer to design an "ultimate weapon." The literal-minded computer proceeded to develop a bomb that if exploded would destroy the entire universe, including the bomb's creators.

Now that's what I call *ultimate*, even if not very smart. I'm going to present you with a more modest ultimate weapon, extremely useful for gamblers and not, I'm happy to report, for destroying the universe. It's called *money management*, and I've broken this particular lesson down into seven important rules.

Rule 1. Some dollars are more valuable than others. Suppose I gave you a chance to make a completely fair even money bet, like flipping a coin, and I offered to pay you 2-1 odds: I'd give you $20 if you won, but you'd only owe me $10 if you lost. You'd jump all over it, as would I and anyone else looking for a favorable investment.

But suppose the only way I'd allow you to make the bet was if you wagered your entire net worth—all your money, your car, your house. Would you make the bet then?

Hopefully you answered "no," because the money you would stand to win isn't as important as everything you already own. Winning would mean increased luxury, but losing would mean poverty, bankruptcy, ruin. Even though the bet itself is favorable, the consequences of losing are too severe.

It's not a very long leap from my "bet it all" example to recognizing that the money you leave home when you go to Las Vegas (money you access with credit or ATM cards) is probably more valuable to you than the money you bring to play with. You leave it home for a reason: Losing it would hurt, while losing what you bring is acceptable. That's why smart gamblers stop and cool off before they hit the ATM.

How often have you started out a trip playing fast and loose, only to tighten up and play smarter as your funds dwindled? You do it because you want to keep playing, and if you lose your whole stake, you're either finished for the trip, or dipping into reserves for more than you'd originally been willing to lose, and neither of those alternatives is attractive.

If you play your best game right away, and don't wait until you're losing badly before tightening up, you'll have money left as your trip draws to a close, and won't need to risk those more "expensive" ATM dollars.

Rule 2. Money you don't lose is just as important as money you win. Most gamblers enjoy winning, but they greatly reduce their chances of winning by the occasional silly bet. In the course of a three-day trip to Las Vegas, or a long poker session, those times where you make bad bets add up and make it much harder to come out a winner.

Rule 3. You can't manage your money well if you don't keep accurate records. If you don't know what's going out and what's coming in, you can't make good decisions about games that may be treating you particularly well or badly.

Most gamblers who fail to keep records do so because they know that they are net losers and don't really want to admit to themselves how much they are losing. Ignorance is bliss, or at least less painful, it seems. Me, I feel better if I know what's happening.

By the way, just because you lose money gambling doesn't mean you need to stop gambling. As I've said before, a great many fun activities cost money, some quite a bit. If your losses are more than you can afford, you probably do need to stop. But for most people, gambling is a manageable entertainment expense.

Rule 3 isn't designed to make you keep records for the IRS, your spouse, or anyone else. It's solely for your own benefit. Although I'm strongly in favor of truth in communication, telling the truth to others isn't part of money management. Make your own decision.

Rule 4. Treat winnings with respect. If you fling money around crazily after you win, you won't have the funds available to offset the inevitable losses.

Rule 5. Learn your point of misery indifference. Almost everyone can reach a point when they're so upset with the evening's losses that they don't care what else happens; usually this turns big losses into monumental losses. If you learn to recognize this "I don't care anymore" point, and to quit then and there, one bad night won't ruin your year.

Rule 6. Keep your bet size small enough to withstand fluctuations (bad streaks). For most games, your bankroll should be at least 50 times the size of your average bet, so if you're betting $10 a hand, you should have a

$500 bankroll. If your bankroll or loss limit is less than 50 times your average bet, you should be making smaller bets.

For slot players, your bankroll should be at least 100 times the size of your average play, and probably much more, because of the nature of slots, where most of the time your money is draining away, and then you're resuscitated by the big win. If you run out of money too fast, you never get that big win.

Fluctuations happen even if you are a favorite in a game (as a blackjack card counter might be), and most of the time you're not a favorite at casino games. When bad streaks happen, they can knock you out if your bankroll isn't large enough to withstand them.

If you don't think fluctuations will happen to you, consider: It is the hope of a negative *casino* fluctuation, a bad streak for the favored casino, that attracts many players. The casino stays in business through such streaks because it has an adequate bankroll. Because you're not a favorite, having an adequate bankroll is even more important.

Rule 7. Life is one long session. Although it's human nature to think in terms of winning trips and losing trips, if gambling is your hobby, you'll be taking quite a few trips in the course of a lifetime.

If you have the strength to honor Rule 7, you will be far less tempted to launch a desperate attempt to win back your evening's losses. And that's very important, because although the occasional comeback does happen, it's far more common for a losing player to keep losing on those nights when things are going badly.

Even if this approach does occasionally deprive you of a dramatic comeback, it will more often deprive you of huge loss. In that sense, Rule 7, like most of my rules, is more of an ultimate defense than an ultimate weapon. If you don't want your personal gambling universe to explode, you'll use the ultimate defense of money management at every opportunity.

Chapter 28

♠

Blackjack
(and Airline Piloting)
Made Simple

If you had just boarded a commercial jet, and the pilot came on the intercom and proudly announced that he had learned everything he knew about flying from a booklet entitled "Airline Piloting Made Simple," something tells me you might develop a sudden urge to see America by train.

Yet despite this admirable display of wisdom, you might eagerly jump into a blackjack game after reading a few words from a booklet called "Blackjack Made Simple." How come?

Okay, I concede that your life is more important than your money, so extra caution makes sense. Mostly, though, I suspect the difference in your approach doesn't stem so much from a disregard for money, as from the view that blackjack is a lot easier than flying a plane, and so a quick lesson is probably enough.

Cautious guy that I am, I like to leave flying to the experts, so I can't make an honest comparison of degrees of difficulty. But I can tell you this much: Playing blackjack well enough to win in the long run is a lot harder than playing passably.

How hard? Out of every hundred people who claim that they count cards, probably one is actually doing it well enough to win. It's a skill that takes practice, and is not a viable part-time pursuit.

If you don't count cards, but merely play basic strategy perfectly, you won't win in the long run, but you will lose slowly enough to be able to enjoy occasional winning sessions and to get some decent entertainment value for your money.

If you don't take the time to learn perfect basic strategy— and that's several hours of study and a bunch more in practice—you should at least learn my Simplified Basic Strategy Table (I'm thinking about changing the name to "Blackjack Made Simple," what do you think?), or you will lose pretty quickly.

Blackjack offers a minor paradox: It's the only casino table game that an expert can beat over the long haul, and yet it's the table game that wins the players' money the fastest, because a non-expert will lose faster at blackjack than at craps, roulette, or slots.

So my first and best advice for blackjack play is, take the time to learn basic strategy. If you are unwilling or unable to do that, you must accept the reality that you are going to lose more quickly than at other games.

If you can accept that reality (either because you're very rich, or because you're going to play very little blackjack in your life), then I can with a clear conscience offer you a few tips on how to play passably without learning full basic strategy.

As a preliminary note, at least as of this writing there is a new kind of video blackjack game called Blackjack Blitz, which offers (in some casinos) excellent rules and payback percentages (99.6 percent with perfect basic strategy, according to the August 1998 *Las Vegas Insider*), and when you combine that percentage with slot club benefits and comps, you have a pretty darn good deal. Before you can take advantage of it, though, you need to know what you're doing, just as you do at a real blackjack table.

Blackjack strategy is based on the dealer's up card. Because the dealer cannot exercise strategy, but instead must hit until he has 17 and then stop, mathematicians can calculate how often he will bust (exceed 21 with) each of his up cards. You don't have to know how they do that— just accept that they can.

The dealer's worst up card (for him) is a five. He will bust it 43 percent of the time (meaning he still makes a hand in the 17-21 range 57 percent of the time!). The six and 4 are almost as bad, the 3 and 2 a little better. Now reverse course: The 7 is his next worst, then 8, 9, 10, and finally the Ace (his strongest).

Why? Think about all those 10-count cards in the deck. When the dealer has a 7 or higher showing, a 10 gives him a non-busting hand immediately. If you want to make it really simple (if a tiny bit inaccurate), just think of the progression as: 6-5-4-3-2, 7-8-9-10-A.

You now know a little about when the dealer is weak or strong, which is tantamount to knowing a little about take-offs but nothing about landings. Your education is seriously incomplete.

Next you must understand your own hand. All hands less than 16 are effectively identical, because the only way they can win is if the dealer busts. You should take a card if you have 11 or less, because you can't bust and you might improve. Taking a card with 17 or more is wrong, no matter what James Caan did in *The Gambler* (besides, things didn't turn out very well for his character in the long run). So the tough decisions come when you have a hand in the 12-16 range (called a "stiff").

Basic strategy tells you exactly what to do, but you're too rich or busy to bother with that, so here's your fake-it strategy: As the dealer's hand gets stronger, you must become more aggressive. As his hand gets weaker, you should play less aggressively.

If you want an incomplete two-sentence strategy, here goes: If the dealer's up card is 7 or higher, and you have 16 or less, keep hitting until you have 17 (or more). If his up card is 6 or less, stand on all stiffs. Note that hands like Ace-4 (worth 5 or 15, because of the Ace's dual nature) are not stiffs, because they can't be busted by one card. For the same reason, hitting Ace-6 and Ace-7 is often right.

Knowing this tiny amount, you now know more than a lot of the players you'll see in casinos. Spend 10 to 20 minutes more with my Simplified Blackjack Strategy Table (Appendix "A") will give you a fighting chance; it sacrifices accuracy for simplicity, but beats the heck out of no preparation at all.

Like the "Airline Piloting Made Simple" pilot, your plane will still crash eventually, but not as quickly as it would have otherwise. Want to fly cross-country? Learn basic strategy...or pack your parachute very carefully.

Chapter 29

♣

The Three Ways to Win

No matter what form of gambling you enjoy, there are three main routes to success:

1. You can be *lucky*.
2. You can be *skilled*.
3. You can *pick the right opponents* (that is, opponents whom you can defeat without needing a great deal of luck).

Let's take a look at these three paths, and what they mean to you.

Luck is a slippery concept. What's luckier, winning a $100 bet when you're a tiny underdog, or winning a $5 bet when you're a huge underdog? Clearly winning the second bet is less likely, but the first is more important.

That's why I view luck as situation specific. It's more important to be lucky some times than others, and more unfortunate to be unlucky in some situations than others. This was never more apparent to me than in the 1984 World Team Backgammon Championships, in Nassau, the Bahamas.

My three teammates and I had rolled our way into the finals, where we met a team comprised of four of the world's top 10 players. Nonetheless, we worked our way into a position where the entire tournament came down to the final game between my good friend Howard Ring and backgammon/bridge expert Kit Woolsey.

Eventually Howard reached a position where if he rolled anything except double ones, we would win the tournament. We were 35-1 favorites, but sure enough, Howard rolled 1-1, Kit rolled a nice reply number, and suddenly we were in an even game. Fortunately, Howard maintained his composure and managed to win from there, so we took the crown.

As my cab sped to the airport (I hadn't expected to be in the finals and had cut it close on the timing of the flight home) I realized then that although I'd heard all kinds of backgammon horror stories ("and then he rolled double sixes five times in a row!") that were far more *mathematically* unlikely than a mere 35-1 toss, Howard's roll, coming at that dramatic point in time, was far more unlucky than a bigger longshot happening in a small tournament or small money game.

Of course, understanding the nature of luck doesn't help one invoke it. Going into a game "planning on luck" doesn't really sound like a promising plan (although sometimes it's the only one available). But you can plan to take advantage of luck, plan to put yourself into position to win *if* you are lucky. And that's where the second path to success comes in—playing skillfully.

As an example, let's invent two craps players, Hank Hardway and Peter Passline. Hank only bets the Hardways (double 2s, 3s, 4s, and 5s), where his disadvantage runs between 9 percent and 11 percent, depending on the bet. Peter only bets the Pass Line, where his disadvantage is 1.4 percent.

Now, let's have a mythical Luck God throw the same thunderbolt at both of them. "I like you," the Luck God booms, "therefore I command that each of you shall be 5-percent luckier than the Laws of Chance decree. Go forth and gamble."

What happens? Hank continues to get hammered. He's "lucky," that's clear enough, winning more than his fair share of bets, but he will still continue to lose, because that lovely 5-percent luck advantage given him by the Luck God isn't enough to overcome his uphill struggle in betting the Hardways.

Peter, on the other hand, has been transformed. Where once stood an underdog now stands a 3.6-percent favorite, a titanic edge that would sink a casino, if he plays long enough.

Peter and Hank were equally lucky, but only Peter won. So when you head to Las Vegas thinking "I'll win if I'm lucky," make sure you add the caveat "and if I play smart." Hank-types certainly win once in a while, but it's pretty obvious that being extremely lucky is going to happen less often than being a little lucky.

Of course, the Luck God, if there is one, probably doesn't spend much time hanging around casinos. I imagine the Luck God is rather busy keeping people from being run over at busy intersections, creating romances, and inducing wicked bosses to retire early.

How can you become more of a Peter and less of a Hank? The more skill the better, obviously, but at the same time most people have no desire to spend a lot of time becoming a gambling expert. It's recreation, not work, and achieving expert level is a lot like work. Even a little bit of preparation can make a huge difference, though. Let's look at the difference between a weekend of playing as an 8-percent underdog, and a 1-percent underdog.

To put this into perspective, you would be an 8-percent underdog if you were:

1. Playing a fairly average slot machine.
2. A craps player who scatters a lot of "Field," "Any Seven," and "Hardway" bets in among the more sensible ones.
3. A rank beginner blackjack player.

You'd be roughly a 1-percent underdog if you were:

1. Playing a 98-plus-percent return slot machine at a casino that had a good slot club.
2. A craps player who bets the Pass Line and usually makes an equivalent size odds bet.
3. A blackjack player with a reasonably good, but not perfect, command of basic strategy.

Let's stick with the names we've been using, and refer to our 8-percent underdog as Hank Hardway and our 1-percent underdog as Peter Passline. How do their weekends turn out, with *average* luck? I'll do the math for you, and we'll assume 16 hours of gambling in the weekend in all scenarios:

If Hank plays the slots, playing three coins on a dollar slot, 300 pulls an hour, he loses $1,152. If he plays craps with an average of $30 in action each roll (a $10 Pass Line bet, a $10 Field bet, and a $10 Hardway bet...this isn't exactly 8 percent but Hank won't make the same plays every time), he gets in about 60 bets an hour, and loses $2,304! If he plays blackjack, averaging a $20 bet, 80 hands an hour, he loses $2,048 (in reality, he probably won't lose this much, because in 16 hours of play the typical novice would learn enough to become only a 3- to 4-percent underdog).

This has been with average luck, mind you. If Hank has a bad weekend, the numbers get worse! Now you see how casinos grind people who don't know what they're doing into hamburger. You've got to be awfully lucky to overcome that 8-percent handicap.

What about Peter? Same games, same amount of action (although Peter will be making different bets at the craps table). At the slots, he'll lose $144. At the craps tables, he'll lose $288. At blackjack, he'll lose $256. It won't take much of a Luck God thunderbolt to turn this into a winning weekend, and even without the thunderbolt, those aren't unreasonable entertainment expenses.

Sounds like one weekend is pretty tolerable, the other pretty terrible. If you're only a 1-percent underdog, you're getting a lot more bang for your gaming buck.

So how do you go from 8 percent to 1 percent? What you're doing right now, reading *Casino Gambling the Smart Way*, is a good start. There are plenty of other good books out there (and plenty of bad ones, so be selective), although most of the good ones are a bit technical for the casual player. Attending one of my seminars (or a seminar by anyone else who is good and who is *not affiliated with a casino*) would sure help. Here are a few quick tips if your trip is next week, though.

If you play slots, play in casinos with good slot clubs and high published rates of return. Play machines in high visibility areas, and if you're playing a progressive jackpot machine, make sure it hasn't been hit lately. The higher the jackpot builds, the better your odds.

If you play blackjack, learn a little about Basic Strategy. You don't have to memorize the whole chart—a lot of the situations don't come up very often. Most people can learn my simplified version of the chart (Appendix "A") in 10 to 20 minutes. And most casinos don't mind if you take the full chart right into the casino with you.

If you play craps, stick to the pass or don't pass bets, and take odds. The Field, the Hardways, and (to a slightly lesser extent) buying the numbers will get you broke quickly.

If you play baccarat, don't bet the tie bet.

If you play roulette, play only at those rare places which feature European-style, single zero roulette, and for the most part stick to the even money bets (like red or black). Because of the "capture" feature of the European game, which gives you a second chance on even money bets if green comes up, the house percentage on even money bets is half what it is on the individual numbers.

If you play anything else...well, you shouldn't be playing anything else! Go play slots, blackjack, craps, baccarat or European-style roulette. In the next chapter, we'll talk about where the third and easiest path to winning comes in: picking the right opponents.

Chapter 30

◆

Picking the Right Opponents

In Chapter 29 we saw how being lucky and being skillful are the paths most people envision when they think about winning at casino games, and how luck and skill are more related than most people realize. Now let's talk about the third path to victory: picking the right opponents.

Some will claim that "picking the right opponents" is really just a subset of "being skillful." I treat it separately because it's an incredibly important subset, and a very different kind of skill than counting cards.

"Picking the right opponents" sounds like a discipline suited only to private games, but that's not true. Casinos are merely opponents who know how to stack the odds in their favor. Casinos are not easy opponents to defeat, but they offer compensations: a fun and exciting atmosphere, they're ready to play whenever you are, you're certain to get paid when you win, and they won't cheat you.

Those descriptions usually don't apply to private opponents, and the last two on the list (getting paid and no cheating) are big improvements over two of the most unfavorable aspects of private gaming.

Nonetheless, it is possible to pick the right casino opponent, and I suggest you devote a fair amount of energy to the choice.

As a starting point, if you know yourself to be someone who plays almost exclusively in the casino where you're staying, then you should pause before selecting a casino based on the room rate they offer you.

Sure, it's nice to get a room for $49 a night instead of $79, but if the games offered are less favorable, and you play a lot or for high stakes, that $30 a night difference is an illusion for two reasons: First, it's tiny in comparison to the amount you're risking at the tables, and, second, if you really are playing a lot for high stakes in one hotel, you'll be getting your room for free anyway.

As an aside, I'm not a big fan of giving all of your business to one hotel, for reasons I've discussed in other chapters. But back to business. How can the games be more favorable at one casino than another? Most people view casino games as essentially interchangeable, and that's what a lot of casinos want you to think. But there are big differences.

If you're a blackjack player, check out the rules of play. How many decks? Fewer is better. Does the dealer hit soft 17? That's a house advantage. Other important player-favorable rules include the ability to re-split pairs, to double down on any first two cards, to double down after split, and to surrender.

In a casino that offers *all* of these favorable rules (which won't happen, except possibly during a special promotion), a good basic strategy player is virtually even money. In a casino that offers none (which *will* happen), you're more like a 1-percent underdog, even with perfect basic strategy—an immense difference. And remember, you're not likely to play basic strategy perfectly. The *average* player adds 1 percent to 2 percent to the house advantage with mistakes; a bad player can add a lot more.

In some foreign countries, the rules are worse. If you encounter a game where blackjack pays only even money, or where the dealer wins ties on certain totals (in Sweden, for example, the dealer wins ties on 17, 18, and 19), run screaming in the other direction.

If you're a slot player, check the slot club payoffs. There are a lot of differences between casinos and I won't cover them all here, but just a little time invested in checking out where you're playing will have a big impact on your results.

The craps differences come mainly in odds play. Casinos offering big odds opportunities are more favorable, *if* they allow you to make a small line bet. The offer of "100x odds" doesn't mean much to most players if they require a $10 line bet, because the 100x odds bet would be $1,000, well out of the intelligent money-management range of most players. But 100x odds with a $1 minimum is a real deal. ("Hundred times odds" means that you can make an odds bet that is up to 100 times the size of your Pass Line bet.)

Roulette games are all or nothing. Unless a casino offers European-style single zero roulette, you shouldn't be playing roulette there, period.

You should also consider playing more at casinos offering short-term promotions, or at casinos that are less strict about comp guidelines. To obtain such information, you can either spend a lot of time walking or calling around to the different casinos, or you can subscribe to a good publication such as the *Las Vegas Advisor* (currently $50 a year; you can call 702-252-0655).

Finally—and perhaps just as importantly—you should pick a casino that's comfortable for you. Maybe that means "no smoking" tables, maybe that means friendlier dealers, maybe that means less glamour and intimidation. The important thing to remember is that not only will you have more fun (and isn't that the idea?), you will also, all else equal, enjoy better results. It's hard to play well, or with self-discipline, if you're in a bad mood.

What about playing against individuals? In casinos that means poker, where the house makes its money by taking a percentage of the pot, or by charging an hourly rate to play. If you're good enough, you can win. I'll offer a guess here, though: You're not good enough to win playing poker in Las Vegas.

Because of those house charges, to win in Vegas you not only have to be better than the other players at the table, you have to be a lot better, and the average Las Vegas player is pretty darn good.

You might be the champ of your home poker game, but moving from your home poker game to a Las Vegas game is not unlike a baseball player moving from the low minor leagues to the major leagues. That's a transition very few people are able to make, and even those who make it usually struggle for quite a while before succeeding.

Tough pros don't play in the lower-stakes Las Vegas poker games, so if you're a home-town champ and want to play, you might be safe in a game with $4 and $8 bets. Anything bigger and you'll probably lose. Also, games with unfavorable house rakes (money taken from each pot for the house) won't have any pros in them, but the unfavorable rake can wipe you out just as surely as a few pros can.

The best bet for winning is a "friendly" (Ha!) little home or club game, be it in poker, backgammon, gin, billiards, or whatever, if you can figure out the skill levels of the players in the game. An advanced intermediate player, playing against low intermediates or beginners, is going to win a lot more money over the long run than a World Champion playing against other expert-level players.

I'm not saying that you shouldn't ever play with players better than you. It's a good, if expensive, way to learn, and the challenge can be fun. But you need to be able to recognize what you're doing, and be careful about how much money you put at risk in these situations. Remember an important saying: if you can't figure out who the fish (weakest player) in a game is, it's you.

One quick pair of tips for poker players: It's okay to play *Limit* poker with two or three superior players at the table, as long as there are also two or three inferior players. You'll take turns carving up the lesser players, and their action is probably worth the hands you'll lose to the better players. But in *No Limit* or *Pot Limit* games, one great player can break you.

The ability to assess opponents' skill levels quickly is probably the most important skill a "private" gambler can have. Your first clue is your opponent's self-description.

My experience is that people who claim greatness are usually not very hard to beat. On the other hand, when I meet someone who says, "Oh, I play a little," I slip into *Star Trek* mode: Red Alert! Shields up! Occasionally the speaker will be telling the truth—he or she plays a little. More often it means you're staring down the barrel of a .44 magnum expert.

Until you develop a good eye for talent, the best gauge of relative skill levels in private games is your results, and that's why accurate recordkeeping is so important. If you're a winning player over the long run, you're probably a little better than the others in the game. If you're a losing player over the long run, there is a reason for it, even if you can't figure out what the reason is.

As long as you're honest with yourself about your results, you will be able to pick the right games. Becoming more skillful takes time. Picking the right opponents yields dividends immediately.

Chapter 31

♥

Say, Is This Here an Honest Game?

There are plenty of reasons why casino gambling offers advantages over home or club gambling: Your game is always waiting without the hassle of setting up; there's no need to clean up afterwards; the casino ambiance is fun; you win money from (or lose it to) strangers instead of your friends; you're assured of getting paid when you win; there's no risk of a hijacking (gamble-speak for a robbery); and it's legal.

But perhaps the biggest reason of all (although knowing you'll get paid when you win is awfully high on most players' lists) is the perception that you'll get a more honest game in a casino. Private game cheats have been around for a long time—archeologists found loaded dice in the ruins of Pompeii.

For the most part, that perception of honesty in casinos is accurate. It's not that casino owners are unusually honest or honorable, but there's one very good reason why they don't cheat—they don't have to.

The legal house percentages give the casino the right to take your money plenty fast. A casino has to be in a bad location or be very badly mismanaged to lose money. So why cheat and risk a legal license to take your money fast, just to try and take it faster?

In fact, cheating would probably be bad for business, because players would come to associate losing with that casino and eventually go somewhere else. Gee, should I go back to that game that skewered me, or check out the tables somewhere else? Not a tough call.

This is why casinos make more money at craps than at roulette, even though roulette has a higher house percentage than most craps bets. People lose too quickly at American-style roulette, so they don't play it much, and in turn the casino doesn't win much.

So it's pretty safe to say that you can rest easy in American casinos. The house isn't going to cheat you. I'm mostly going to leave foreign casinos out of this discussion, as they present very different questions. But casinos have been closed for cheating outside our shores, and I had some pretty eye-opening things happen to me in some small casinos in the Czech Republic three years ago.

You pays your money, you takes your chances, I think, when you play in a small casino in a developing nation. I don't think America was any different in its developing days.

Getting back to America, you'll note that I said "the house" isn't going to cheat you. That's not the same thing as saying you won't get cheated, because the house isn't the only entity capable of cheating you. There are two other candidates: dealers and your fellow players.

Why would a dealer cheat? Usually not just to impress his employers, although I heard a funny story recently about a Money Wheel dealer who was so grateful the casino had hired him that he was cheating the customers just to "thank" his new employer. The casino fired him when it found out.

Most of the time when a dealer "cheats" you he isn't really cheating at all, but rather just making an honest mistake. *You* try standing for eight hours with all those buzzers and bells and flashing lights and see how mistake-free you can deal. After a long hard day it's easy to see how a dealer could look at your blackjack hand of 3, 9, 2, and 4 and think you had 17 instead of 18, so you have to stay alert.

By the same token, that tired dealer can also read 3, 9, 2, and 4 as 19 instead of 18, and pay you when you should not get paid. Do what you will in those circumstances. In casinos, I usually accept the payoff, because I figure they make mistakes in their favor that I miss from time to time, and also because pointing out a mistake can embarrass a dealer and possibly get him or her into trouble. In a home game, I always correct mistakes. Make your own call.

Honest dealer mistakes are why you should never make a bet without knowing your fair payoff. This comes up most often in complex games like craps or roulette. The math on odds bets can get wearying for dealers (I've especially noticed problems on "Don't Pass" and "Don't Come" odds bets), so I think it makes sense to bet an amount on which you can calculate your correct payoff easily.

On the other hand, I know people who like to constantly shift the size of their bets, and to bet odd amounts like $35 or $55, just to try to trap the dealer into making mistakes. The ethical considerations involved here aside (and I think they're real), you have to be pretty fast with math and very alert, or a strategy like this could easily backfire.

Although I would be willing to bet that more than 99 percent of dealer errors are just errors, it is possible to run into a cheating dealer. Normally this happens when the dealer is trying to cheat the house, rather than you specifically, and is doing so by letting a partner or confederate win unfairly, and then splitting up the profits later. When a dealer does that, his or her table results would suffer, so he or she has to cheat some of the regular customers so that the overall results are just about what the casino would expect.

How can you spot a cheating dealer? It's tough, because the number of ways a good cheat can nail you is almost infinite. Obviously if a dealer keeps making mistakes in the house's favor, you need to pick yourself up and move.

Probably it will be much more subtle than that, so just apply my Basic Gambling Rule 4: If something keeps happening, it is probably happening for a reason, even if you don't know the reason. So if you find yourself losing a lot at one table, move. It can't hurt, and it might help.

Sometimes dealer activity stinks, but it isn't clear whether it's right to call it cheating. I walked into a smaller Las Vegas casino once, played blackjack for a while, and then in a moment of weakness took my pile of chips over to a craps table, where the shooter was in the middle of his roll. So I plunked everything (about $150, a big bet for that casino) onto the table as a Come bet.

The shooter immediately rolled an eleven, so I was a winner. But the boxman (dealer) claimed the bet hadn't been made in time and refused to pay me. I left and never returned. Was I cheated, or the victim of an error combined with poor customer service? For my purposes, it didn't matter. The casino had lost my business forever.

Your fellow players are a much more likely source of cheating. The bad apples realize the risks inherent in trying to cheat the casino itself, and so set their sights on a more appealing target: you. We'll next discuss a few of the ways they go after your hard-won chips.

Chapter 32

♠

Coppers
and
Robbers

In Chapter 31 we discussed the rare instances when you might get cheated by a casino employee. This time we'll talk about a much more common problem: getting cheated by fellow players.

I'm going to confine this discussion to casino cheating, because covering non-casino cheating would take an entire book, just to get started. I can't even really cover casino cheating in any detail here, but we can touch a few key areas where increased awareness might save you a bundle.

The most elemental casino cheating isn't really cheating at all, but stealing. Watch those chips! Pickpockets have an easy time of it in casinos, where thanks to what I call "the dance of the living dead," most people walk around so focused on the gambling they just finished, or the gambling they're on their way to do, that they seem half-zombified, and frequently collide with one another.

As a result, it's easy to get used to people bumping into you. But if you do, you can easily fall victim to a pickpocket. I favor clothes with Velcro-sealing pockets for casino trips.

You're not safe at the tables, either. "Chip coppers," as they are called, can reach past your stack and take a chip without you ever noticing. Sometimes they're good at sleight-of-hand, and sometimes it's just adhesive.

I read about one pit boss who was so suspicious of a woman player that he glued a stack of chips together and set a shill playing next to her. When her adhesive-coated hand made for the top chip, she came away with the whole pile, calmly set it down, and left the casino, never to return.

Chip coppers aside, you're pretty safe at blackjack tables, because the layout isn't confusing, and at roulette tables, where each player has his or her own color chips. Craps can be a bit more dicey, if you'll pardon the expression, especially when a table is very full. Dealers are usually good at physically positioning your bet so they can figure out it's yours, but you still should keep track of your bets.

Because rack space can get tight, and it's very difficult to watch the dice and your chips simultaneously, chip thieves can have a field day at busy crap tables, although dealers will try to look out for you. I once went to the Bahamas with my friend Theresa and was enjoying a winning run at a craps table when I noticed her taking chips out of the rack and putting them in her purse.

I knew with certainty that she wasn't stealing them (she's very honest and anyway I'm pretty sure she was richer than me), but rather was making sure that I kept some of my winnings. But I had fun watching the dealer follow her efforts and try to catch my eye with an expression that said, "Hey, buddy, do you see what's happening here?" Although tempted by the opportunity this created, I gave the dealer a nod, so he didn't call security.

I'm not a big slot-player, but I have this recurring fantasy/nightmare about hitting a mega-jackpot and having someone try to shove me aside and claim that it was his machine (I wonder...does that dream make me an optimist or a pessimist?). Although the video surveillance cameras usually record who is playing, I'm sure it has happened. In fact one 19-year old who won a million dollar jackpot and who then quickly switched places with his dad, so they could collect, was denied payment because the surveillance camera showed who was actually playing the machine.

Your best defense against jackpot claimers, aside from evil-looking tattoos and a mean countenance, is to make lots and lots of noise the instant you hit a jackpot. Fortunately, most players have no problems following this advice.

A more realistic slot danger is theft by fellow players or thieves who walk through casinos looking for opportunities. People who play more than one machine, and who in turn leave money in the tray at the bottom of more than one machine, are extremely vulnerable to this kind of theft.

The poker tables hold the biggest dangers, although paradoxically I think they're just about the safest place for your chips. I (and most other players) leave my chips on the table all the time, to go to the restroom or wherever, and have never had a problem. I wouldn't even think about leaving my chips at a craps table, though. It's a different atmosphere. I know players who are comfortable leaving chips at blackjack tables—I'm not.

It's very easy to fall prey to more sophisticated kinds of cheating at poker tables. Although the home game fear of a cheating dealer is virtually gone, you can still be cheated by sharpers who mark cards (although dealers and other players are good at spotting this and taking the cards out of play). A much greater danger comes from partnership play.

If two players agree in advance to combine their winnings or losses, and set out to cheat others in the game, your only defenses are a suspicious nature and an alert cardroom manager. Myself, I would count on the suspicious nature.

How do partners cheat a game? Not with the clumsy Three Stooges trick of passing aces back and forth under the table. Instead, they apply money pressure to others in the game. For example, Partner #1 bets, Partner #2 raises, you call, #1 raises and #2 re-raises. You fold, figuring that if #2 can keep re-raising, he must have something awesome. Regardless of what they had, they split up your money.

My view on partnership cheating is not universally accepted. No less an expert than my friend Phil Hellmuth, Jr. (who as a baby-faced 24-year old in 1989 was the youngest player ever to win the World Series of Poker and who is today widely regarded as the world's top tournament poker player) doesn't think partnership cheating is a big danger, because, as he told me when he was reviewing this chapter, "You can just wait until you have pocket aces (the best possible starting hand in Texas Hold 'Em), let them try to trap you between raises, and take both of them."

In other words, if you're a smart, conservative player who doesn't play too many junky hands, the extra partner raises don't hurt you. The danger from partners drops dramatically and indeed you may actually profit from their efforts. However, for those of us who don't play as well as Phil (which is practically everyone), and who tend to play too many starting hands, I still think it's worth paying attention to unusual raising patterns.

Perhaps an even more important lesson is to play higher-quality starting hands, where Phil's philosophy of using that quality hand to collect money from both of the attempted cheaters not only defeats the cheaters, but also means improved results against the overwhelming (and I do mean overwhelming) majority of your opponents who aren't trying to cheat. So in a weird way, facing opponents who are trying to cheat you might improve your results, if you're savvy enough to make an adjustment that should probably be part of your game all the time.

Another variation on the same problem can come up when the two cheaters employ secret signals that tell each other what they have, even if they aren't trying to push you out of the pot. Suppose you have a pair of Aces, cheater #1 has a pair of Kings, and cheater #2 a pair of Jacks. Cheater #2 drops out because he knows his friend has a better hand, and so you win less money than you should have. Without the cheating, you'd have collected from two players who had good hands while you had a great one. With the cheating, you only collect from the player with the Kings. I'm oversimplifying, but I hope you can see that "getting cheated" isn't limited to losing a hand that you should have won. If partnership play means you won less than you should have, you've been cheated.

As Phil suggests, there are ways of turning the tables on this kind of cheater, too (just imagine the fun you can have if you intercept their signals). But as they used to say on *Hill Street Blues*...be careful out there!

There aren't too many other ways you can get cheated in casino poker games, although in private games you're at risk from dozens of different cheating methods. Increased player awareness has helped cut it down some. Another high-powered poker friend of mine (who has also won the World Series of Poker) once said of the private poker "circuit" in the 1970s, "If you weren't cheatin', you weren't tryin'." And you thought all you needed to know was not to draw to an inside straight! (Actually, if the pot odds are right it could be a good play, but that's another lesson.)

Maybe I'm just too suspicious. In 1997 I returned to a private poker game I used to play in regularly when I lived in Atlanta, and observed a change: The players, tired of answering each others' constant questions about what dealer's choice game was being dealt (a variation of my *Dance of the Living Dead* theory, no doubt; see the Glossary for more), had purchased several large brass numbers, which they placed in the middle of the table. Number 1 meant Hold 'Em was being dealt, Number 2 meant 7-Card Stud, etc.

As soon as I sat down with my old friends, I asked, "Do you mind if I flip this number over (to the non-shiny side)?" When they asked why, I pointed out that anyone dealing the cards could flip a card past the shiny brass number and read what the card was. We quickly tested this and I called five cards in a row correctly. There were a fairly large number of sheepish glances around the table. "We've been using this for months," one embarrassed-sounding player explained.

"Well, probably no one was doing anything," I said. "I just don't see any reason to take a chance." And they all agreed. I still wonder if there was at least one player who was less than thrilled about my special guest appearance in the game.

I have a hard time understanding the thought process of the cheating player. People who would never consider armed robbery or burglary or even shoplifting will cheat without hesitation, as if it were just part of the game, instead of the theft that it is. Sometimes I've played in games with known cheaters because they were such bad players that they lost anyhow. But in general I believe in the old maxim, "Lie down with dogs, wake up with fleas." If I know someone is a cheat, I don't want to play cards with him, and I don't want to associate with him away from the table, either.

Sorry to create all this distrust of your fellow player. Cheating doesn't happen all that often, but it can sure ruin your day when it does. So you can add one more item to the already long list of reasons why you need to stay aware and alert when gambling in casinos. We have met the enemy, and it is us.

Chapter 33

♣

The Sucker's Only Even Break

It was actually Edward Francis Albee, not W. C. Fields, who first said, "Never give a sucker an even break." Casinos have been doing their best to follow this instruction ever since, but they actually offer one even break, if you're open to it.

Before you jump into this chapter, though, I must offer a few warnings: There's a little math here, the chapter is entirely about craps, and the information offered is a bit more technical than almost anything else offered in the book. So if you have never played craps, you might want either to skip this chapter until sometime after you've seen a live craps game, or to go slowly, and be patient with yourself.

When you go to a craps table and bet the Pass Line, you're bucking a house edge of 1.41 percent. Not bad (and certainly better than most of the other bets available at a craps table or in a casino), but enough to grind you into dust if you play long enough.

Once you've made that Pass Line bet, though, the casino gives you an absolutely even break. The "odds bet," which is the wager you see people placing behind their initial bet, if the shooter rolls a 4, 5, 6, 8, 9, or 10 (these are the "point" numbers, which the shooter must roll again before rolling a 7, to win). The other first-roll numbers (2, 3, 7, 11, and 12) decide the bet immediately and so there is no chance to make an odds bet.

The payoffs on odds bets are fair—no advantage to the house, no advantage to the player. If the point is four, for example, the odds bet pays a fair 2:1. The payoff is fair because there are three rolls ("ways") to make a four (3-1, 1-3, and 2-2), while there are six ways to make a seven (6-1, 1-6, 5-2, 2-5, 4-3, and 3-4).

All the other rolls become irrelevant, once a point is established. Because the only rolls that matter are 4 and 7, and because 7 is exactly twice as likely to come up as 4, a 2:1 payment is fair.

The casino is indifferent to your making an odds bet because over the long run, no money will change hands. But *you* shouldn't be indifferent, because odds betting is the smart way to play.

Suppose, for example, that you want to bet $50 a roll (just an example—there are places where you can bet 50¢ a roll, and the same logic will apply). You can bet the $50 in one of two ways: either all on the Pass Line, or part of it on the Pass Line and part of it as an odds bet.

In some casinos, your odds bet can't be any bigger than your Pass Line bet. This is a "single odds" game, and you can do better, but let's start here. If you bet the whole $50 on the Pass Line, the house percentage is 1.41 percent. But if instead you bet $25 on the Pass Line, wait for a point to be established, and then bet $25 as an odds bet, you reduce the house's effective edge to about 0.85 percent on your $50 wager.

If you find a "double odds" craps game, you can make your odds bet twice as large as your Pass Line bet (note that you don't *have* to bet this much; it's just an option). So in this game you would bet $15 on the Pass Line, and then make a $30 odds bet. This reduces the house edge to about 0.60 percent.

If you find a "10 times odds" game, you would bet $5 on the Pass Line and $50 (or $45, if you want to stick to exactly $50 total) on the Pass Line, and the house edge reduces to about 0.18 percent. That isn't an even break, but you're coming darn close. And 10x odds games aren't all that unusual anymore.

There are now casinos offering 100x odds and even unlimited odds! In a game like this, the house percentage is low enough that you can just about pay for it with pocket lint.

So there you have it, and you can have it without worrying about the math: The best deal in any casino is a minimum Pass Line bet coupled with a maximum odds bet. But before you head to the tables, it's extremely important to know that you shouldn't bet more than you're comfortable with just to lower the odds.

For example, if a 10x odds table requires a $5 minimum bet, you might not want to make a $50 odds bet simply because you're not comfortable having $55 in action every roll. Although the odds on your wager are reasonable, even a little bad luck could put you down $500 in a few minutes.

In other words, *don't equate good percentage betting with good money management.* Staying within your means is *far* more important than shaving a bit more off the house percentage. If that means a $5 Pass Line bet and a $15 odds bet, so be it.

Your goal when you walk up to a craps table is *not* to reduce the house percentage to the absolute minimum, then. Your goal is to reduce that percentage to a minimum, *within the parameters of a comfortable bet size.* That's a crucial difference.

Why do casinos come close to offering you an "even break" with 10x odds? Competition. If the casino next door offers 2x odds, maybe they can lure you in with 10x odds, just as they might with their cheap buffet. They also know that few people will take full advantage of the 10x odds and, to do so, they have to be willing to put a lot of money on the table, a potentially dangerous habit.

If you take advantage of odds bets to the extent your bankroll allows, you'll be getting a pretty fair deal from the casino, no matter what Edward Albee or W. C. Fields said. Just remember the priority that money management deserves; if you don't, on your next trip to Las Vegas, you'll decide that on the whole, you'd rather be in Philadelphia.

Chapter 34

♦

Taking a Shot
at Low Risk:
The Casino Tournament

One of my favorite moments in the first *Rocky* movie comes when Rocky tells his local bartender that by fighting Apollo Creed, he's at least "taking a shot" at a better life. The bartender, clearly comfortable in his little world and uncomfortable with Rocky's efforts to climb out of it, pours a shot of whiskey and says, "Hey, you want me to take a shot, I'll take a shot," and gulps the whiskey down.

A lot of gamblers like the idea of "taking a shot" at The Big Score, but recognize that the only realistic way to try to win a large sum is to put an equally large sum at risk. Winning $10,000 isn't so very hard, if you're willing to risk $10,000. If your bankroll is only $500, winning $10,000 at regular table play or the slots is very unlikely.

To me, trying to win big money by risking big money isn't taking a shot: It's just high-stakes gambling. I think "taking a shot" implies a chance at huge gains while not risking as much as you stand to gain. In other words, going to Las Vegas with $500 in your pocket, planning either on winning $10,000 or losing the $500, is taking a shot. Not a very likely shot, true, but a shot nonetheless.

It's kind of the difference between a 19th-century duel where you stand 20 paces from your equally well-armed opponent, with each of you firing simultaneously, or using Danny DeVito's tactics in *Romancing the Stone*, where he drove furiously away from his pursuers and shot the gun out the sunroof, without bothering to slow down or aim or indeed do anything that would slow down his escape efforts. Danny was literally taking a shot, but sure wasn't going to risk his hide to do it.

The best casino equivalent of Danny's tactics is the gaming tournament. It's even better than what Danny tried, because you can aim quite carefully, and it lets you take a shot at big money while keeping your risk quite small and manageable.

Although casino tournaments can be found in almost any game played in a casino—blackjack, craps, roulette, slots, keno, poker—there are two basic types of casino tournaments, and it makes a big difference which kind you enter.

Type A, the kind I prefer, involves your plunking down an entry fee, and ending your risk then and there, because the tournament is played with special "no cash value" tournament chips that are meaningful only during the tournament. For $100 you might be given $500 or $5,000 worth of chips; the dollar value assigned doesn't really mean anything. The chips are merely a way of keeping track of how you do, relative to the other people in the tournament. You can't use them anywhere except in the tournament.

For the $100 entry fee, you thus get to take a shot at a first prize that might well be $5,000 or more, depending on the number of entrants. If 100 people enter, the casino has a prize pool of $10,000 to distribute to the winners (less whatever the casino holds out for its profit; this varies from 0 to 20 percent, depending on whether the casino views the tourney as a money-making device, or a way of attracting players to the casino for other gaming).

Type B, the riskier kind, involves plunking down a similar entry fee, *but* you are playing with real chips. Risk is still limited, because you can only buy the real chips at certain times, and in certain amounts, but the amount you're risking is less clear, and you can face some difficult on-the-spot money-management decisions. Let me give you an example:

The first blackjack tournament I ever entered was a $50-entry Type A tournament at the Flamingo Hilton. For my $50, I was given $300 in tournament chips, and was taking a shot at a first prize of $3,000 (second was $300 and third was $100).

The format was simple: Players sat at standard tables of seven players. In each round the seven players played 30 hands, and the two players with the most money after 30 hands advanced to the next round. The maximum bet allowed was $200. The chips were turned in after each round so everyone started anew with $300 in the next round.

Well, with one hand to go in the second round, I had $400, and there was one player with $750 and another with $650. Excluding the remote chance of a blackjack, the only way I could possibly advance, assuming the leaders played it smart and conservative (and betting before me, they did, $5 each), was to make a maximum $200 bet and then either double down or split if I had a pair. $600 would do me no good at all; I needed more. I had to get all $400 into action and hope I could turn it into $800.

I was dealt a 10 and a 3 for the unlovely total of 13, and promptly doubled down...and now you can see one of the big differences between a Type A and a Type B tournament. I wasn't risking a darned thing with this "crazy" play. Finishing with $0 or $600 meant exactly the same thing: a seat on the sidelines for the third round. Happily, the dealer gave me a 6, turned over a 17 of his own, and I went on to win the tournament.

If this had been a Type B tournament, I'd have had a hard decision to make. Doubling down on 13 is a horrible play in money blackjack. In a Type B tournament, not only would I have been faced with the need to make an uncomfortably large bet of $200, but also to risk another $200 at bad odds. Worth it? Maybe, if the prize money were big enough (and close enough: this was only the second round, out of four)...and maybe not. A difficult and potentially expensive decision.

So, although Type B tournaments are also fun ways to take a shot at big money, they're not as desirable as Type A tournaments. Before entering a Type B, try to figure out what kinds of bad bets you might have to make, and when it would make sense to make them (in the last round only, for example, when the equity of the prize money looms near).

What makes tournaments so desirable in the first place? Although in a sense you're playing against the house, you're really playing against other people like yourself, who are easier to beat than the house. As other individuals get knocked out, you advance. *You don't have to be better than the house, or to beat the odds. You just have to come closer than other people trying to do the same thing.* It's not uncommon to see the "winner" of a blackjack table finish with less money than he or she started with, especially if the dealer was hot.

The most common tournament of all? You might be surprised: slot tournaments, where the ability to spin the reels as quickly as possible is pretty much all that matters. Casinos love these because they train participants to play the slots fast, and casinos make more money when slot players play quickly.

So if you're interested in taking a shot at a big win, and don't (Heaven forbid!) want to gamble with the rent money, try a tournament. The winner also gets a trophy, and the pleasure from displaying it often lasts a lot longer than the prize money does...and a lot, lot longer than a shot of whiskey.

Chapter 35

♥

Table Games: The Next Generation

That slick *Star Trek: The Experience* attraction at the Hilton isn't the only Next Generation in Las Vegas. If you haven't visited a casino for a while, you might be in for a surprise the next time you stroll through the table games area. While you'll still find your old favorites, you'll also find a whole new generation of games like Spanish 21, Let It Ride, Caribbean Stud, and, even your childhood favorite, War.

I got a little misty-eyed the first time I happened upon War in a casino, because it was a game of War, played on an airplane with my father when I was 7, which first hinted at my future career. When dad went to the lavatory, I stacked the deck so that I had all the high cards and he had all the low ones.

To my knowledge I'd never even heard of stacking a deck at that point in my young life, but upon his return I won battle after battle until, about halfway through the deck, Dad started furrowing his brow and noticing that chance seemed to be favoring the younger Glazer rather strongly.

I hadn't developed a poker face yet, so his first inquiry brought forth a burst of laughter from me, and he put away the cards grumbling something about a future I would have in the law, if they didn't hang me first.

Well, I practiced law for three years before I decided that playing backgammon for a living was more socially useful, so Dad turned out to be a bit of a prophet, even though that was the last time I ever stacked a deck of cards (unless you count one memorable game of strip poker and I don't think I'll recount that here).

Anyway, getting back to War, Spanish 21, and the like, the recreational gambler certainly has a wide range of new choices. Why have casinos gone to the expense of purchasing all these new tables when the old games had such nice, built-in advantages?

Why do you think? You don't suppose it could be some silly reason like *more profits*, do you? Gosh, we've penetrated their strategy already. So let's look behind that strategy and try to figure out why these new games will generate more profits.

As a starting point, casino players are slowly and gradually getting a little better at the old games. Fewer craps players make Field or Hardway bets, most blackjack players have learned not to split fives, and most people have learned to stay away from roulette entirely.

The other side of the same coin involves the public's lack of knowledge of correct strategy for the new games. The body of literature available on Caribbean Stud or Spanish 21 is tiny and weak compared to that available on the older games and, as a result, very few players understand these games.

Because most people don't know that the house advantage on a game like Caribbean Stud is about 5-percent even with optimal strategy, they jump right in and play.

Notice that I said "with optimal strategy." Who knows the optimal strategy? Not too many people, at least not yet.

And there is the big reason for the new games, and the one thing that they pretty much all have in common: *They give the player a chance to make a mistake*, something that a player can't really do with a slot machine, or even at a roulette table (unless you count sitting down and playing as the mistake).

Casinos make a lot of money on blackjack, even though it is well-established that a true expert can beat the game, and that a talented amateur will lose very slowly. Why? Because for every expert and talented amateur playing, there are 20 not-so-talented amateurs playing, and an inexpert blackjack player will lose very quickly.

So even though the casinos were making lots of money at blackjack, they hated the idea of losing occasionally to an expert, and so one day some bright soul got an idea: How about some new games that offer the "good" part of blackjack (the chance to play poorly and lose quickly) without the "bad" part (the chance to win if one plays brilliantly).

Now that's what I call *thinking*, at least if you're a casino executive.

Why are players flocking to these new games? Because most of us want entertainment on a Las Vegas trip, and the new games certainly offer that. Even the process of figuring out a strategy is entertaining, if you don't mind losing while you're doing the figuring.

It's also nice to be able to play badly without other players at the table making faces at you. Someone who hits a hard 16 when the dealer has a 5 showing will draw disdain, disgust, and often even anger from other blackjack players, especially if in hitting the 16 the player takes the dealer's bust card.

But when no one really knows quite what to do, the criticizing and unwanted advice drops to a minimum. Cool! Who wants criticism on vacation?

Indeed, this whole new collection of games reminds me a bit of the games Chevy Chase faced as Clark Griswold when brother-in-law Randy Quaid took him to a smaller casino in National Lampoon's *Las Vegas Vacation.*

"Now, Clark, the games in here ain't like the games they got in them regular casinos," Randy advises him. And the duo wanders into a minefield of hysterically funny games, like Pick a Number Between One and Ten, Coin Toss, Rock-Paper-Scissors, ("Dealer has rock, pay paper") Guess Which Hand, and...War!

Although these games are all familiar to the excited Chevy, he (surprise!) winds up losing the last of his money there. The scene offers an important lesson for the recreational gambler. Chevy got excited because the regular casino games had already cost him his entire bankroll and he figured the new games could hardly be any worse. They were.

In case you haven't seen the movie, I won't give the rest away. They must have worked with a good gambling consultant because it is truly worth a rental as an educational video that could be renamed "Mistakes Not to Make Next Time You're in Las Vegas."

Speaking of mistakes, playing any of the new games for high stakes comes to mind. They're fun enough, so a little play at low stakes can certainly be worth the cost, but if you play too long, or for too much money, your bankroll will have about as much of a chance as Chevy did at Rock-Paper-Scissors, or my dad did in that sky-high game of War.

Except the casinos don't have to stack the deck, because they've already stacked the odds. If the games in the new section ain't like the games they got in them old sections, you can be pretty sure some casino manager knows why.

Chapter 36

♠

Sports Betting,
Swamp Land, and
Other Good Investments

I pretty much quit sports betting in my mid-20s, when I realized that despite my enormous knowledge of both professional and college sports, my historical betting results indicated the best system I could play would be to make my weekly selections and then bet the other way.

Actually, the defining moment came during the 1982 Sugar Bowl game, when I had made a huge bet on the University of Pittsburgh and their star quarterback Dan Marino, to beat the University of Georgia. I was certain Pitt was much the better team, and I was even getting two points, which meant I would win my bet even if Georgia won by a point, or if the game were to end in a tie. I was watching the game at my friend Tom Holder's house, with a few other friends.

With 42 seconds to go in this "sure thing" game, Pitt trailed by three, and faced a fourth down and five yards to go from Georgia's 33 yard line. A successful field goal would have tied the game and won my bet for me, but at the 33 yard line, a field goal is 50 yards long, and that's no sure thing. Pitt disdained the field goal.

"Great!" I thought. "A quick 10-yard pass for a first down, and then a field goal, and I win!" Except that Marino dropped back to pass and then launched not the short pass I wanted, but a long bomb toward the end zone.

Although the pass was only in the air for about four seconds, time has a way of slowing down during a crisis, and in the half-hour or so that the ball *seemed* to remain in the air, I calculated that the swing between winning and losing this bet meant that about 10 percent of my annual salary was riding on whether some 19-year old kid caught one pass, and I decided this was so silly that whether he caught it or not, I was quitting sports betting then and there. Yes, it was a *long* four seconds.

He caught the ball, and the celebration that ensued in Tom's living room greatly exceeded that which took place on the field. But I stuck to my resolve and gave up regular sports betting. Good thing I didn't promise to become a priest or something.

Oh, I'll still make a bet occasionally, when a challenge to my manhood is issued, or when an opportunity like the 1992 major league baseball All-Star game comes along (more on this later), but years of record-keeping and nervous Saturday and Sunday afternoons had set the stage for my sudden Marino Bomb Decision, and my days of regular betting were done.

So why, if I knew so much about sports, was I having so much trouble winning? It's called "the vig."

The vig, or vigorish, is sports slang for the bookie's 11:10 advantage—a 10-percent commission that bookies charge on losing bets. Say that Michigan is favored by 7 1/2 points over Notre Dame. The bookie (or as is becoming increasingly more popular, the Las Vegas casino Sports Book, or offshore Internet gambling Web site) allows me to pick whichever side I want. If I bet Michigan, Michigan has to win by eight or more. If I bet Notre Dame, I win if Notre Dame wins, or if they lose by seven or fewer.

I can pick either side of the pointspread, and the bookie doesn't care which, because when I bet $100 on Michigan, I win $100 if Michigan "covers" (wins by eight or more), but I lose *$110* (the $100 plus the 10-percent commission) if they don't. So in an afternoon where I win five $100 bets and lose five $100 bets, I don't break even. I'm down $50. If I go 4-6, I'm down $260; if I go 6-4, I'm up, but only $160. That's a serious uphill battle.

Sparing you the math, it turns out that just to break even against the vig, a bettor has to win 52.38 percent of his or her bets. If I win 52 percent of my bets, I'm a long-term loser.

So here I was, a guy who had a real job (I was still a lawyer then), who read the sports section each morning and watched a lot of games on the weekend, trying to defeat professional betting lines set by people who had been doing nothing else for 20 years and whose sources of information would put Woodward and Bernstein to shame, and if I didn't beat them by six bets out of every hundred (53-47), I was going to get hammered.

No, that doesn't sound like a good way to make money. And there are other hidden costs in sports betting. If the bookie goes out of business (it happens) and you don't get paid when you win, you've been playing a "might lose, can't win" game. The new offshore Web sites aren't necessarily any more reliable than the neighborhood bookie; if you decide to bet through one, check out a site like www.theprescription.com, which rates offshore casinos according to their reliability.

Let's look a little deeper. Why do you want to bet on sports? It's almost certainly not to enhance the enjoyment of watching the game, because the bet adds stress. It might create interest in a game that you otherwise don't care about. But if you don't care about it, why do you want to start caring about it?

I think most sports bettors place their bets for the same reason I used to: They feel that their sports "expertise" means they will be favorites to win. So they feel like they are investing wisely, but when most bettors look at their long-term results, *if* they do so honestly, they realize they're not winners.

At that point, a bettor might start to look for help, in the form of a "tout service," an operation run via a 900 number or a subscriber Web site that offers "winning selections" for a fee, sometimes a very hefty one.

Frequently these tout services offer "guarantees," like "if you don't win, you get the next month of picks free!" Gee, that sounds valuable. If your advice is worthless, I get lots more of it. Even if the guarantee is "money back if you lose," the tout service is risking nothing, while you are risking your hard-earned dollars.

Often tout services give away free selections to entice people to join. An unethical one can simply tell half the free players to bet Michigan, and the other half to bet Notre Dame. Half of the callers thus come away convinced that the tout service is brilliant, and they sign up.

Like most people who sell "guaranteed winning systems," if touts could really pick 70-percent winners, they'd be out betting, not selling their system. Some services do offer good information, but the vast majority do not. And even if you find a good one, the cost of the service means you have to win 55 percent or 60 percent of your bets, and that's almost impossible.

Besides, wasn't the whole point of sports betting doing it because *you* knew a lot about sports? If you pay for someone else's picks, that reason goes out the window, and you're simply making unfavorable bets based on questionable information.

Occasionally you may stumble across a true opportunity, but these are rare. Before the 1992 baseball All-Star game, I was watching ESPN when they reported live that the baseballs for the game were special edition balls, made just for the game, and that the seams on the baseballs were lower than normal. This had literally just been announced, only two hours before game time.

Although ESPN didn't explain what lowered seams would mean, I knew this would have an immense impact on the game. The raised seams on a baseball are what give a fastball some movement, and give a curveball a lot of movement, making these pitches harder to hit. Without regular seams, the pitchers would be at a big disadvantage, and the game would be high-scoring. It made sense to me: The recent All-Star games had all been low-scoring, and fans like to see hitting in an All-Star game, so the baseball powers-that-be had taken some covert corrective action.

I quickly called a friend: What was the "Over-Under" number on the game? Over-Under is a bet on the total number of runs scored in the game by both teams; usually the number is somewhere around 7 or 8. If "the number" is 8, an Under bettor wins if the final score is low, like 4-2, and an Over bettor wins if the score totals 9 or higher. It doesn't matter who wins, by how much, or if the score was really low (like 1-0) or just barely low enough (like 4-3).

I don't recall the precise number, probably because I wasn't that interested. I would have bet Over unless the number was something impossibly high like 15, which would have meant the bookies already knew about the baseballs. I bet my friend's limit on Over (I didn't have a regular bookie anymore and gaming Web sites hadn't happened yet). I think they scored 8 runs in the first inning, and the final score was 13-6. It was the easiest bet I had ever seen. But we're talking about a once-a-decade kind of opportunity here, the equivalent of being the first to know that Michael Jordan would be missing a game. Informational advantages like that are very rare and they don't last long.

Until or unless you come across that sort of opportunity, I think you'll find that your sports betting results probably aren't all that different from mine. It's just too hard to beat the vig.

Now, if you can honestly say that betting money on the games increases your enjoyment, even when you lose, then keep on betting. You're paying for entertainment, just as you pay for entertainment in other forms of gambling.

Similarly, as a once-in-a-while proposition, like someone who comes out of the woodwork to bet on the Super Bowl or the World Series, sure, go have some fun. Just as with other forms of gambling, if you don't make a lot of bets, the small house percentage isn't a major obstacle.

But if you feel lousy on your losing days, and they outnumber your winning days, your quality of life probably isn't being enhanced by sports betting. You're probably doing it because you like gambling so much you're not satisfied with an occasional trip to Las Vegas—and that's a danger sign of a potential problem gambler.

Sports bettors are particular vulnerable to doubling up after losing (a terrible idea in any form of gambling), because they don't have to dip into their pockets for cash or chips to make the big bet. They just call the bookie, or get on the Internet, and make a bigger bet. Monday Night Football betting action is very heavy, because of the number of weekend losers who are trying to get even with the Monday Night game.

There are risks in all forms of gambling, of course, but the risks in sports gambling are particularly high. I think you'll be doing yourself a favor if you tread very carefully here.

Part Six:

Closing Thoughts

Chapter 37

♣

Andy's Enlightened Casino: A Bad Idea?

Late in 1997 I ran a casino night for my friends at the Esalen Institute, in Big Sur, California. Esalen is a gorgeous New Age health spa and seminar center on the Pacific coast where I once lived for a couple of years, and I put this little party together as a gift for my friends there.

This was not a conventional casino night, though. Because Esalen is a place where people try to learn a bit more about themselves and hopefully grow a little, I called the room "Andy's Enlightened Casino," and made the games "enlightened" by changing the rules so that the odds favored the player, rather than the house!

I was able to do this because no money was involved. No one paid anything to play and at the night's end, the chips were exchangeable only for donated prizes. So it didn't matter if everyone won. All that mattered was each player's total, relative to the other players' totals.

At my blackjack tables, blackjack paid 2-1, instead of 3-2, and I offered every favorable player rule ever invented, from early surrender to more than one card on split aces, as well as a few I created, like "player blackjacks and multi-card 21s cannot be beaten or tied."

At my craps table, Pass Line bettors did not lose on an initial roll of 2 or 3, and I rounded odds bets up to favorable, easy-to-pay payoffs. Field bettors had the "5" added to the list of rolls on which they won (an immense difference!). As stickman I also tended to leave Hardway bets in place even if the natural number came up.

As you might imagine, the players enjoyed great success under these rules. Very few lost their stake and most multiplied it quickly. Virtually everyone had a great time. And while that was my goal, I now wonder how much of a service I was doing for my friends.

Even though I took every possible opportunity to tell the players that the rule changes I had instituted were important and that they should not expect to duplicate this success in a real casino, I wonder now if I was creating an unfair excitement level that would encourage these players to go to Las Vegas and try their luck.

"What's wrong with that?" you might ask. "You teach gambling for a living, Andy, so what's wrong with encouraging people to go to Las Vegas?"

Well, I don't want to encourage people to go to Las Vegas, at least not people who aren't going there already. I've seen too many players lose more than they bargained for. I teach casino self-defense to people who already enjoy gambling, because if you're going to gamble, you might as well do it well, keeping losses to a minimum and winning more often than the typical visitor.

Whenever someone tells me that they don't gamble, I tell them, "Congratulations. Keep it that way." People seem surprised because of my line of work, but America already has 5 million problem gamblers and I don't want to add any more to the list.

Probably the warnings I gave at the Enlightened Casino were enough to create a sense of caution about real Las Vegas trips, but my experience is that people often have selective memories when it comes to gambling, and will conveniently fail to focus on any information that gets in the way of their gambling. So I worry a little about creating quite as much gambling excitement as I did in the Enlightened Casino.

The casino equivalent of my Enlightened Casino is a winning trip your first time to Las Vegas. This kind of beginner's luck can be very dangerous as it creates an impression that the games are easy to beat, or that you are a magically lucky player, or the like, and the mental image of first-time success can remain powerful even after several later losing trips.

Even good (or potentially good) gamblers can be seduced by selective memories and/or wishful thinking—two items that I've taken to calling the Dark Side of the gambling Force.

When I was 13 years old I was already 6'3", so I was able to play blackjack for a while in a Las Vegas casino on a family vacation. I lost $20, a lot of money for a 13-year-old in 1968. When we left town, my sweet and loving mother gave me the $20 back, and so my memory of getting knocked about was transformed into a highly fictional, "Well, I guess I broke even."

At a conscious level I knew I'd "broken even" only because my mother had given me a gift, but at a subconscious level, all the sting of my loss was gone, and, thus empowered by the Dark Side, I continued gambling. Fortunately for Mom and her conscience, it turned out that I was a pretty good gambler whose seduction by the Dark Side was only temporary.

I think you can see the risk of early success, or even early lack of failure. If your own early gambling experience was very positive, and things haven't been going so well lately, you might want to ask yourself some hard questions about whether you've been clinging to images and impressions that are no longer supported by the facts.

If you can do that, or indeed any other kind of honest self-assessment about what you like about gambling, how much you spend on it, and how much fun you get out of it, you won't get hurt much in casinos, and you won't have to go to an Enlightened Casino to win. You, and your own personal enlightenment, will be a winner before you ever walk in the door.

Chapter 38

♦

Gettin' Out of Dodge: The "Boom-Boom" Strategy

Your weekend trip to Las Vegas is coming to an end. You've already checked out of your hotel and in 15 minutes you're going to take a cab to the airport. You've had fun, you've played rationally and at a reasonable stake, and you're down $160.

For a lot of people, just moving right on to that cab is the best possible plan. They've tempted the winds of chance and fate for a weekend and spent $160 on entertainment, not a bad deal at all.

Some of us—and you have to understand both yourself and your gambling budget, before you can decide if you fit in this next category—might want to consider finishing the trip a little differently, with a bit of flourish that I call "Boom-Boom."

I first developed my Boom-Boom approach many years ago, at the end of a trip like the one described here: lots of sensible, low-stakes gambling, which left me up $300 for the weekend. Not bad at all, but I was in the mood for something more dramatic, so I decided to take the weekend's profits to a craps table, plunk them down on the Pass Line, and try to make two straight passes (Boom-Boom). If I made it I'd have $1,200, and if I lost I'd be even for the trip.

Chance was with me, and I left with the $1,200, although it wasn't easy. I rolled an 11 on my first throw and so had $600 immediately, but then I rolled a 5, and it took at least 20 rolls before I rolled another 5. By the time I finally made my point the dice felt like they weighed about 80 pounds each and I could barely stand. So it really wasn't Boom-Boom, but rather more like Boom-argh-argh-argh-argh-Boom.

So when the dealers looked at me and said, "How about one more time?" I drew in what little breath I had left and said, "No thanks, I'm gettin' out of Dodge." And that's just what I did.

So here you are, down $160, which as I've said isn't bad at all if you had fun, and you're thinking, "Gee, I came so close, it would have been nice to win."

If you were making lots of small ($5) bets throughout the weekend, then as a $160 loser, you really didn't come very close. You played smart, but you lost 32 betting units (32x5=160). And that makes sense, because it's hard to win when you make thousands of bets into a house percentage.

But when you're only going to make two bets into a house percentage, it's not so hard to win.

I can already hear my pro gambler friends screaming: "Life is one long session, Andy! If you make two large bets at the end of every trip, after hundreds of trips your large bets will have been ground down by the house percentage."

True enough, if you're going to make hundreds of trips. But most of my readers aren't going to make hundreds of trips in a lifetime. A few dozen is more like it, maybe less.

So here you are, down $160, and you're thinking, "I'd be willing to risk going home down $260, if I had a decent chance at a winning trip." Okay. Take $100 out, and go make a bet. Don't play blackjack because you might have to split or double down and then your commitment to risking only $100 has to change. Roll the dice or head to the baccarat tables.

If you lose, *go home.* Do not try another big bet. *Leave.* You're down the $260 that felt acceptable. If you get suckered into another bet and lose, you're down $360 and it's starting to hurt. When you make another bet, you're not playing Boom-Boom: You're just another guy making big bets, and if you were making little bets all weekend, you don't have the kind of money to be "just another guy making big bets."

If you don't have the self-discipline to walk when you lose, don't try Boom-Boom.

Now, if you win your initial $100 bet, let it ride, and if you win that $200 bet, take the $400 off the table and go home. You're now a $140 winner for the trip, instead of a $160 loser. If you're feeling really rambunctious, you can try for a "Boom-Boom-Boom," which would make you a $540 winner, but it's awfully hard to watch the dealer whisk your $400 bet away when you lose.

By the way, if you decide to play craps for your Boom-Boom, following my youthful lead and just plunking it all on the Pass Line isn't quite optimal strategy. You're better off complicating matters a bit with a small Pass Line bet and a larger odds bet.

Boom-Boom works if you've had a small trip result, plus or minus, and you want to reward yourself for solid, stable play with one dash of danger and excitement before you leave. If you fit the criteria, and if you really can walk away when you lose (which will happen 75 percent of the time), then it's a little like indulging in a chocolate sundae after a healthy meal—not so good if you do it often, but okay as a once-in-a-while treat.

Why does Boom-Boom work only if you've had a "small trip result?" There are two components here: "Small," and "trip result."

As to the trip result component, Boom-Boom is most definitely not a mid-trip strategy. You need literally to be on your way out the door, or else you're just another guy making big bets (see above), with plenty of time left to get into trouble.

As to the "small" part, when you've already won a lot, there's no need to risk any of it in the last 15 minutes. You're already happy and going home a winner—why mess with success?

When you've already lost a lot, not only will you almost certainly need a one-in-eight chance Boom-Boom-*Boom* to get even, but more importantly, your emotional state is probably a little unstable. A vulnerable moment is no time to start suddenly messing with big bets. Just head on out, and get 'em next time.

Chapter 39

♥

The Professional Gambler's Paradox

On more than one occasion I've written that people who take casino trips to improve their personal balance sheet, buy a new car, or upgrade their lifestyle are unrealistic. Sure, winning happens. We wouldn't go to Vegas if it didn't. But gambling isn't a smart path to riches.

"Wait just a minute!" cries the reader. "Your own bio says that you're a 'former professional blackjack, backgammon, and poker player.' So either you made money consistently by gambling, Andy, or you're a liar! If you did it, why can't I?"

Well, it's true that I've made lots of money in all those games, supported myself at each at different times in my life, and, what's more, I have quite a few friends who have done or are doing the same thing.

Nonetheless, you'll note that the bio says "former" professional player, and my reason for that wasn't a losing streak (though like all players I've had them). Mostly it was a lifestyle choice, but it was also a recognition of something that I now call the Professional Gambler's Paradox.

To make a living as a professional gambler, you must possess each and every one of a long list of traits. You must be: very smart and very quick (not quite the same thing), self-disciplined, self-confident, courageous yet cautious, analytical, and mathematical; able to assess other people's psychology; cool under pressure; able to recover from seemingly unfair blows; and have the physical and mental stamina to play long sessions without a significant drop-off in your skills.

If you have each and every one of those traits, while also having access to capital (your stake) and a reputation for honesty (more important for some games than others), you can make a living as a professional gambler. If you lack one or more, sooner or later you will start losing or at best win very little. So what's the problem, if you *can* claim all of those traits?

Here's the rub: If you really possess all those traits, while you *can* make a living as a professional gambler, you can make a lot more money doing something else. Trading stocks or commodities on an exchange floor is one example, and there are quite a few other careers where someone meeting the criteria could excel.

It's a paradox because anyone who meets the criteria can make more in another career, and anyone who doesn't won't make it. The paradox isn't complete: It's possible that you could enjoy gambling so much that you view a sacrifice of money, prestige, and potential for improving the lives of others acceptable.

But it's not for me anymore—I want to do something more useful—and not for most casual gamblers.

Perhaps you're thinking along slightly different lines. You don't want to be a professional gambler, but you do want to be a highly successful amateur—someone who wins consistently on trips to Las Vegas. It stands to reason that if a professional can make a living at it, a talented or well-trained amateur can be at least reasonably successful, right?

Maybe. It depends on your approach, and on what you like to play. The cagey gambling veterans among you probably noticed something important about the list of games I played for a living: blackjack, backgammon, poker. These are games that combine skill and chance.

You do not see games like craps, roulette, slot machines, the money wheel, bingo, or keno on my list, for a very good reason: No one can beat the house at those games in the long run (let's leave one special kind of slot—video poker—in a separate category; we discussed it in Chapter 26).

There is no such thing as a "professional craps player" or a "professional roulette player," unless that person is a cheat. Those games are pure chance, and publicly traded corporations don't build casinos costing hundreds of millions of dollars because some guy who gets a tip from his Uncle Fred can come up with a system that will whip the casino at craps.

On the other hand, it's equally important to understand that just because you can't be a professional craps player doesn't mean you can't be a very *good* craps player. Most of the pure chance games provide the opportunity for players to lose either slowly or quickly. A good player keeps the house edge to a minimum. It is actually possible for two people to be placing the same size bets at the same craps table and for one of them to be mathematically likely to lose *100 times as fast* as the other!

Nonetheless, even the good player rates to lose in the long run—although by playing well, the good player has a much better chance of coming out a winner in the short run, for a three-day or three-week or even three-month stretch. It can and does happen, and it's a blast when it does.

Just remember that your winning streak isn't your birthright—it will end. If you decide that your winning streak means you are a "lucky" craps player, and bet heavily on your next trip, you're likely to give back everything you won previously, and more.

The games on my own play list are a little different. Blackjack can be beaten by a card counter. Although it is tough—much tougher now than it used to be—it can still be done. Backgammon and poker fall into a completely different category, because in those games you aren't playing against the house, but rather against other people.

Backgammon isn't a casino game, but big money tournaments are held in casino towns. Poker is played in casinos, but the house makes its money by charging the players rent for their seats. In small stakes games, the casino rakes a percentage of each pot. In larger games, players pay an hourly fee. The house doesn't care who wins, as long as the table stays full.

So in games like these you *can* win in the long run if you're good enough. If you enjoy the other games, your goal should be to reduce the house edge to a minimum through smart play. That's true of every casino game, even slots. Most people play so badly that even if they get lucky, they lose anyway. By playing well, you'll reduce your losses when you do lose, and you'll win much more often.

Chapter 40

♠

The 10
Basic Rules
of Gambling

I didn't invent any of these rules, and there are certainly others I could have added. But these strike me as the 10 most important gambling lessons I've learned over the years. When you combine them with my Top 10 List of Gambling Mistakes (found in the next chapter), you have a pair of lessons that, if you follow them, will almost certainly mean *tremendous* improvement in your gambling results and, perhaps even more importantly, will almost certainly mean that you won't have that one bad night that ruins weeks, months, or years of solid, acceptable results.

It's a good idea to review this page and my Top 10 List of Gambling Mistakes before any gambling trip.

1. If you can't (or won't) be honest with yourself, sooner or later your gambling is going to lead to trouble.

2. If you gamble with money you can't afford to lose, you *will* lose.

3. If you don't know who the fish (sucker) in the game is, it's you.

4. If something keeps happening, it's probably happening for a reason, even if you don't know what the reason is. So treat trends you dislike with respect; you can't get badly hurt if you assume a negative trend will continue. On the other hand, treat positive trends with caution; there might be a good reason for the trend, but you might just have been lucky, and a too-strong belief in continuing good fortune has been the ruin of many a gambler.

5. Money you avoid losing has just as big an impact on your finances as money you win.

6. The odds win. You can buck the percentages for a little while, but over the long run the percentages determine who wins. Anyone who thinks otherwise is invited to my weekly poker game.

7. Don't assume that everyone else is as honest as you. Watch out for cheaters, and always cut the cards.

8. Luck is the residue of design. The more prepared you are, and the more you study your game of choice, the luckier you'll become.

9. Gambling when you're emotionally unstable, tired, or intoxicated, is not gambling, it's donating.

10. You don't have to win it all back tonight. Life is one long gambling session, with frequent breaks for work, sleep, love, and other hobbies. You'll have another chance later.

Chapter 41

♣

The Top 10 Gambling Mistakes

With thanks to David Letterman, for so many laughs along the way...

#10. Spending more on dreaming than necessary. You buy the right to dream about winning the lottery with your first ticket purchase. After that, you're just making bad bets.

#9. Gambling more than you really want to, just to try to earn casino comps. Casinos give free rooms and meals to people who gamble at high stakes for long periods of time. They do this because they know it gets people to gamble more. Risking thousands of dollars (which is what you're doing by making $25 bets for an hour or two) just to earn a free dinner is usually a bad idea.

#8. Refusing to accept or savor the taste of victory. Winning sessions put a real bounce in your step, but most players keep right at it after a big win, leaving themselves no chance to feel like a winner. If you take a break after you've won, the casino can't take away the time you felt like a winner, even if they eventually win your money back. If you stop gambling for the trip, you get to feel like a winner until your next trip.

#7. Gambling when you have just come into a lot of money. Immediately after they've won or inherited a lot of money, or received a Christmas bonus or other windfall, most people don't treat money with the respect they normally do, and are vulnerable to losing a big sum that they might later wish they'd held onto. When Lady Luck stops smiling on them and they hit a losing streak, they don't have the money available to keep playing.

#6. Gambling when upset, tired, drinking, or under the influence of drugs. Too obvious even to discuss. Gambling a lot immediately after you arrive in town is closely related, because you're probably both tired from travel and excited—and that makes you vulnerable.

#5. Gambling big just to impress someone else, especially a dealer. No matter how big you're gambling, the dealer has seen much bigger action. The dealer might act impressed, but it's only an act. If you are gambling big to try to impress someone else, consider that you might be better off impressing that person with your common sense, and spending some of the money you're risking directly on him or her (buy an expensive dinner, take a trip, etc.).

#4. Increasing the size of your bets during a losing streak. Long losing streaks happen occasionally, and if you increase your bets on the assumption that the streak must end soon, you might run out of money before the laws of chance swing back your way.

#3. Confusing a good percentage bet with good money management. Even if the odds are fair or reasonable, if you bet too large a percentage of your bankroll, you might not be able to play long enough for the odds to assert themselves in your favor.

#2. Gambling past your point of misery indifference. Once they've lost a certain amount, most people eventually reach a point where they are so upset they no longer care what happens to them that night, and a big loss then turns into a staggering loss. When you find yourself saying something like, "I don't care" or "I deserve it," go home—immediately!

And the Number 1 Gambling Mistake...

Assuming that gambling is all luck. Even in pure-chance games like slots and craps, a few minutes of study can reward you with an immense difference in the amount you win, or the amount you fail to lose. All slots are not created equal, and neither are all craps bets.

Chapter 42

♦

Rounding 3rd and Heading Home, Wrapping Up This Little Tome

If you've been reading this book sequentially, by now you know a *lot* more about gambling than most of the people you will see in casinos, and probably quite a bit more than your family's version of Uncle Martin (quite a few families have one; mine is mentioned in Chapter 7), although he'll never admit it, of course.

And even though much of the advice I have offered has been cautionary, you now sit at a very dangerous moment in time: the "a little knowledge is a dangerous thing" moment.

I've seen this phenomenon more times than I can count. Someone buys a blackjack book, glances at it briefly, and then heads to the tables, confident that his or her new, scientific gaming method will bring riches. The funny thing is, often the person hasn't even really read the book! Sometimes merely the act of buying it is enough to trigger this false self-confidence, for some reason.

I guess I shouldn't say "for some reason." I guess I should go ahead and say "The Reason," because it's the same for almost all gamblers, and I will include myself with the that vast majority, even though by now I've learned to resist its seductive powers.

The Reason is this: *We want our gaming reality to fit our gaming dreams and hopes.* We *want* the mere act of purchasing the book to be enough. We *want* to be the magically lucky player who is rewarded for his or her good life with amazing good fortune. We *want* the bad breaks we suffer in other areas of our lives to be counterbalanced with good luck while gambling. We *want* our craps system to be right.

We want it all so much, we're often willing to ignore reality and hard evidence, and go right on pretending, go right on not looking carefully at our behavior.

Casinos know this, of course. Why do you think casinos are growing more and more into adult fantasylands? Although many people gamble because they like the tension that "action" brings, many more go to Las Vegas because it is an escape from their daily reality. And when they are in the middle of an escape from reality, the last thing that most people want to do is look at their fantasy through reality-colored glasses.

Only you can decide if you're willing to tone down your fantasy world sufficiently to play smart. I think the rewards of winning more often and losing less on the losing trips are an ample reward, but that's me. You may want something very different out of Las Vegas and that's fine. More to the point, I'm not the one to judge whether or not it's fine. I'm not the one who has to face your job, your responsibilities, your wife, your husband, or who has to make your way through the world. So I can't possibly judge what the right escape for you is. It's your life.

Instead, what I want to do is help you understand your motivations, help you look, if only for a little while, at your gambling with a very clear and rational eye. Just long enough so that you can really decide what you want, what's best for you in the course of one trip, and what's best for you in the course of a lifetime of entertainment and risk.

Hopefully, I've written this book well enough so that you will enjoy pulling it out every now and then for a re-read, because even though I've tried to avoid getting overly technical, it would be unrealistic to assume you absorbed every lesson the first time through. If that's too ambitious, Chapters 40 and 41 summarize many of the more important principles I've touched on in the book, and a quick re-read of these before a gambling trip will probably be helpful.

Gambling is certainly not the only area where human beings indulge in wishful thinking. It's not even the most dangerous one. People who drive drunk, or who take outrageous health risks, are certainly risking more than the people who put their cash on the line. But money is still pretty important to most of us, and the risk that makes gambling so exciting can sometimes have painful consequences, if wishful thinking blinds us to reality.

So I ask you, as someone I care about, to consider bringing a little less wishful thinking to your gambling. I ask you to consider bringing a little more awareness to your fantasy world. I ask you to consider treating yourself and your gambling funds with the same kind of respect and consideration you would treat someone you love very much. You deserve it. You're doing your best.

Speaking of doing your best, just because you lose when you go to Las Vegas, you are not "a loser," at least not in the more general life sense where people get labeled as losers or winners. I don't really like such labels, but if you have to use them, a loser is someone who consistently loses where someone else would win, someone who messes up a potentially winning situation by underperforming.

Someone who loses reasonable sums in Las Vegas is not a loser under that definition, because the house percentages dictate that the player will lose. Virtually everyone who plays the pure-chance games loses in the long run, so don't get down on yourself and call yourself a loser just because the expected happens.

One last request: If you liked this book, if it brought you a smile, taught you something useful, or added a little something to your day, consider passing that positive energy along to someone who needs it, a friend, a relative, a stranger, whoever. That would be a nice "thank-you" for me. And who knows, the good karma might help on your next trip to Las Vegas.

Good luck, fair winds, and may the Force be with you.

Appendix A

♥

Andy Glazer's
Simplified
Blackjack Strategy

Important note: The following strategy table is not perfect!!! It is a *simplified* version of basic blackjack strategy, designed to be easier to learn for people who don't want to take the time to learn the complete basic strategy chart. Some of the advice is slightly (but only slightly) wrong: I have sacrificed precision in favor of ease of learning.

If you're going to be playing for significant money, or for a long period of time, *I strongly recommend learning the full chart* instead of this one. If your choice is between guessing or learning my simplified table, my table will help a lot! Finally, please don't take my "the table isn't perfect" statement as a license to play hunches. You should only ignore the following advice if your studies of the full chart tell you to do something else!

You will lose many hands even when making the right play, tempting you to go with hunches. If you avoid this temptation, you'll win more; the *right* play isn't always a winning play. Some hands, like hard 16, are net losers no matter how you play them, but with the right play, you'll lose less, and make it up on your good hands.

Your Hand	Simplified Advice
Nine or less	Always hit—you've nothing to lose!
10	Double down against the smaller cards (2-9); hit against 10 or A.
11	Always double 11!
12-16	Stand against 2-6, hit against 7 or more.
17 or more	Stand.

Pairs

2s, 3s, 6s, 7s	Split against 2-6, hit against 7 or more.
4s, 5s, 10s	Don't split. (A pair of 5s is 10, so double down against 2-9!)
8s, Aces	Always split 8s and Aces!
9s	Split against 2-9, stand against 10, ace (standing vs. 7 is good, too).

"Soft" Hands (Hands that include an Ace that can't be busted by a hit)

Ace and 2 thru 6	Hit (double against 5 and 6 if you remember).
A-7	Double against 2-6, stand against 7, 8, hit against 9, 10, A.
A-8, A-9	Stand; no need to mess up a nice 19 or 20.
Insurance	Never take insurance!

The dealer's weakest upcard is a 5; he busts that 43 percent of the time. Note that even with his *worst* card, he *still* makes a hand in the 17 to 21 range 57 percent of the time! The full ranking of dealer upcards, from weakest to strongest, is: 5, 6, 4, 3, 2, 7, 8, 9, 10, Ace. There is a big jump between the 2 and the 7 (the 7 is a much stronger card); that's why the dealer upcards 2 thru 6 are often treated differently from those 7 or higher.

When you split a pair, you're doing three important things:

1. You're changing the value of your starting hand (for example, when you split 8s, you don't have to play that rotten 16; if you split 10s, you've destroyed a very nice 20).

2. You're doubling the amount of money you have in action (nice against a weak upcard, not so nice against a 10 or Ace).

3. You're creating a new starting hand (nice if splitting 9s; awful if splitting 5s).

Appendix B

Blackjack Basic Strategy Chart

Your	Dealer Up Card										
Hand	2	3	4	5	6	7	8	9	10	A	
= 8	H	H	H	H	H	H	H	H	H	H	
9	H	D	D	D	D	H	H	H	H	H	
10	D	D	D	D	D	D	D	D	H	H	
11	ALWAYS DOUBLE ELEVEN!										
12	H	H	S	S	S	S	S	S	S	S	If *surrender* is
13	S	S	S	S	S	H	H	H	H	H	allowed, surrender
14	S	S	S	S	S	H	H	H	H	H	hard 16 against a
15	S	S	S	S	S	H	H	H	H	H	dealer 9, 10, or A,
16	S	S	S	S	S	H	H	H	H	H	and 15 vs. 10.
17	ALWAYS STAND HARD ON 17 OR GREATER!										
2s	H*	H*	SP	SP	SP	H	H	H	H	H	*If double-down
3s	H*	H*	SP	SP	SP	H	H	H	H	H	after split is
4s	H	H	H	H*	H*	H	H	H	H	H	allowed, split
5s	D	D	D	D	D	D	D	D	H	H	these hands. If not,
6s	H*	SP	SP	SP	SP	H	H	H	H	H	hitting is slightly
7s	SP	SP	SP	SP	SP	SP	H	H	H	H	better.
8s	ALWAYS SPLIT 8s!										
9s	SP	SP	SP	SP	SP	S	SP	SP	S	S	
10s	NEVER SPLIT 10s—STAND ON 20!										
As	ALWAYS SPLIT ACES!										
A-2	H	H	H	D	D	H	H	H	H	H	
A-3	H	H	H	D	D	H	H	H	H	H	
A-4	H	H	D	D	D	H	H	H	H	H	
A-5	H	H	D	D	D	H	H	H	H	H	
A-6	H	D	D	D	D	H	H	H	H	H	
A-7	S	D	D	D	D	S	S	H	H	H	
A-8	ALWAYS STAND ON SOFT 19!										
A-9	ALWAYS STAND ON SOFT 20!										

Key: S=Stand   D=Double Down   SP=Split Pair   H=Hit

Important notes:

1. Don't deviate from the chart just because you have a hunch. If you're counting cards, that's different, but if you were really a counter, you wouldn't need this chart!

2. Don't play in a casino where the rules are bad (doubling down allowed only on 10 or 11, for example).

3. Be willing to take a break if something throws you off. The casino will always be there.

4. Remember that the chart offers the *right* plays, but not necessarily *winning* plays. That is, when you are dealt a 16 vs. a dealer Ace, your hand is going to lose most of the time however you play it. But if you play correctly, you will *lose less* in the long run, allowing you to make money on your good hands, like 11, and come out a net winner.

5. This chart is neither secret nor magical; possessing it won't guarantee winning. If you follow it and have average luck, you will come very close to breaking even. If you follow it and have bad luck, you will lose, and if you have good luck, you should win.

Appendix C

Glossary

If you've gotten this far and noted the irreverent tones I favor, you've probably guessed that the Glossary won't read like a typical Glossary...and that's a good guess!

While quite a few entries are relatively straightforward definitions of gambling terminology, I've also included quite a few "Andy Glazer terms." These are words or phrases that I invented for use in my seminars and have used in the book, and which I believe will help the reader remember certain important concepts.

Because I invented these entries, be wary of using them in conversations with friends, even experienced gamblers, who are unlikely to know what you man when you refer to "TEF" or the "Dance of the Living Dead." Fear not; any "Andy Glazer terms" are clearly identified as such.

There's a lot of useful information in this Glossary, I think. Read on, enjoy, and as always...be careful out there!

—A. G.

100x odds. Shorthand term for a craps game, which allows the player to make an odds bet 100 times larger than his or her Pass, Don't Pass, Come, or Don't Come bet.

Action. Gaming term used sometimes as a synonym for betting, and sometimes as a synonym for the amount bet.

Andy's Enlightened Casino. Play-only casino night where the rules of the casino games are changed to make the players favorites over the house. Great fun but potential danger for players to believe regular casino gambling would be equally easy.

Bankroll. The amount of money that you have decided to make available for gambling. Note that just because you might have other funds available to you (the rent money, your retirement fund, money friends might be willing to lend you, etc.) you should not consider these part of your bankroll should you run out of gambling funds.

Basic Strategy. Computer-derived, commonly accepted system for playing casino blackjack well, without a counting system.

Biased Roulette Wheel. Often hoped for, never found: a roulette wheel that through time and neglect has fallen out of balance, favoring some numbers over others. Players often mistake random short-term fluctuations for wheel bias, and then lose huge sums of money betting that the fluctuation will continue.

Big Score. A gambling win large enough to change the player's life in some way.

Big Six/Big Eight. Terrible craps bet offering even money if a 6 (or 8, if you bet Big Eight) comes up before a 7. It's a terrible bet because all you need do is ask the dealer to "place the 6" (or 8) and receive a much better return. But novice craps players don't always know this, or are sometimes intimidated and/or afraid to talk to the dealer, and the Big Six/Big Eight is located right near the edge of the table, for easy access to the timid. Thankfully, many craps layouts are now designed without spaces for Big Six/Big Eight.

Black Chips. $100 chips.

Boom-Boom Strategy. System for making a large bet immediately before departing a gaming town and letting it ride once if you win.

Boom-Boom-Boom Strategy. System for making a large bet immediately before departing a gaming town and letting it ride *twice* if you win. Because of house percentages, more than twice as likely to fail as a Boom-Boom strategy.

Bust. In blackjack, to have your hand exceed 21 (and thus lose). If both you and the dealer bust, the dealer wins, which is the primary source of the house advantage at blackjack.

Bust out. To go broke, or lose one's bankroll.

Call. In poker, to match the size of the previous bet. You will sometimes see signs at craps or roulette tables saying "no call bets." That means the house does not accept verbal wagers (the reason for this is clear; it would lead to all sorts of disputes and collection problems). You have to put your chips down to place a bet.

Card Counter. A blackjack player who keeps track of the cards that have already been dealt and who then applies this knowledge to his or her play, adjusting both bet size and playing strategy in accord with the count. For every 100 people who claim to be a card counter, probably one can really do it. Even those who can do it are eventually victims of their own success, becoming barred from all casinos.

Casino Tournament. Usually excellent form of casino gambling where the player gets a shot at big money for a relatively low risk.

Checks. Synonym for *chips*.

Chip Copper. A thief who steals your chips by taking them from your stack or tray when you aren't looking.

Chips. Casino tokens, usually made of clay or plastic, used as money substitutes for table game play. Chips are colorful and look like toy items for a reason: Casinos want you to think of chips as toys and not as money. This is not all that different from the phenomenon of credit card money seeming less real than cash. Somehow, signing a charge slip for $60 doesn't hurt the way peeling off three twenty dollar bills does. Most players' level of betting would be much lower if they had to pull $10, $20, or $100 bills out of their wallets or purses every time they had to make a bet. If you know that you tend to bet a little more than you should, you'll probably find it a useful exercise to imagine a pile of real money sitting in front of you, instead of a pile of colorful chips. A somewhat more concrete way of approaching the same exercise is to exchange your chips for cash more often than you need to. If you keep reminding yourself that these cute little tokens represent the same money you fight so hard to protect the rest of the time, you'll probably do a little better at holding onto it.

Come Bet. Identical to a Pass or Pass Line bet, except that it can be made at any time other than when the shooter is first coming out (which is when you would make a Pass bet).

Comped (Getting). Having the casino pay for your food, room or airfare because of the amount of money you bet for an extended period of time.

Come Out or **Coming Out.** In craps, a shooter's first roll when new to the game, or after a successful pass. If this roll is a 4, 5, 6, 8, 9, or 10, it becomes the shooter's "point."

Comps. "Free" food, beverages, rooms, or airfares given to gamblers whose play "earns" them these perks. I put the word "free" in quotes because the comps are only given to players who give the casino considerable action, and who as such figure to lose far more than the value of the comps. The casino does not require the player to lose; all they want is player action, figuring that if the player gives enough action, sooner or later he or she will lose. Free drinks are not usually considered comps because all players are entitled to them as soon as they sit down; a bottle of expensive champagne would qualify as a comp, though.

Cramden, Ralph. Jackie Gleason character on *The Honeymooners* who often tried to achieve financial freedom by investing in "get-rich-quick" schemes of very dubious wisdom.

Crapspeak. An insider language used by experienced Craps players, usually in an attempt to impress dealers or novice players with their expertise. As with most forced efforts to impress others, this one usually only works with the easily impressed.

Croupier. The dealers in a roulette or baccarat game. Usually there are two in roulette, one who runs the game, spins the wheel, collects losing bets and paying winners, and a second who re-stacks chips and acts as an assistant. In baccarat there are several assistants.

Dance of the Living Dead. Andy Glazer phrase (adapted from Rodney Dangerfield in *Caddyshack*) referring to many gamblers' tendency to lose focus, or focus too much. You can see this in action walking through almost any casino—watch how many people seem to walk rather aimlessly, completely unaware that someone might be behind or in front of them. This creates a great many collisions and near-misses, and is a fascinating subject for people-watching during your gambling breaks. It's easy to see how it happens: the rush of gambling excitement, or depression over losing, the multiple gambling options available (Should I go to that machine over there? Or maybe that one from yesterday? Or maybe...) mixed together with thousands of flashing lights, buzzers, and bells, creates a kind of zombie-like trance. Think the casinos try to encourage this? Naaaaaahhhh.

Dime. $1,000. Why not just say one thousand? Sometimes gamblers prefer that the non-gamblers around don't know how much they're betting.

Dodge, Get Out Of. Leaving a casino or game while the getting is good.

Don't Come. Identical to a Don't Pass bet, except that it can be made at any time other than when the shooter is first coming out (which is when you would make a Don't Pass bet).

Don't Pass. Craps bet where the player wins if the shooter rolls a 2 or 3 on the first (come out) roll, loses if the shooter rolls 7 or 11 on the first roll, and ties if the shooter rolls 12. If the shooter rolls any of the other numbers (4,5,6,8,9,10) on the first roll, the Don't Pass bettor wins if the shooter rolls a 7 before rolling the original (come out) roll a second time.

Double Down. In blackjack, to double the size of your initial bet after you have received your first two cards and have had a look at the dealer's up card. You receive one and only one more card after doubling down, one of the reasons why doubling down on a total of 9 isn't so favorable; you really hate it when you're dealt a 2.

Drop (The). The amount that the casino takes in from players who buy chips; also used to refer to the amount of money "dropped" into one or more slot machines by players. At most table games, the players' cash is literally dropped into a box, which is removed by casino security and replaced by an empty box on a periodic basis. Casinos have a percentage figure they expect to make on each drop, and the figure is *not* the house percentage at the game. For example, a casino might expect to win 70 percent of the drop at blackjack, not because the house percentage edge is 30 percent, but because players will recycle their chips through the system again and again.

Equity. An important and complex concept involving value, as in the value of your position. For example, someone who has reached the finals of a $5,000, winner-take-all tournament can be said to have some equity in the tournament; how much depends on how many people are in the finals, and whether their skill levels are similar. If in this example we assume five equally skilled players in the finals, each of them has an equity of $1,000. They haven't won anything yet, but their one-in-five chance of winning $5,000 is worth $1,000. Similarly, if a hotel sponsored a 100 player tournament, charging a $100 entry fee, but awarding only $8,000 in prizes (deducting 20 percent for expenses and hotel profits), the average player's equity, or worth, at the start of the tournament would be $80. As players are eliminated, the equity of the remaining players grows. Understanding your equity in a gambling situation is particularly useful if you want to hedge your bet and sell part of your position to a third party. For example, our player in the $5,000 finals might go to a friend and say, "I'll sell you half of whatever I win, for $500." Because the two friends can calculate the equity to be $1,000, selling half for $500 is fair. The risk is now shared. The player in the tournament is no longer facing a $5,000 or nothing situation—he or she will win either $500 (the friend's payment), or $3,000 ($500 payment plus half the $5,000 prize).

Esalen Institute. Gorgeous New Age health spa and seminar center in Big Sur, California. No gambling or gambling seminars, but a great place to explore yourself, expand your horizons, or get a massage. Call (831) 667-3000 for a catalog.

European Style Roulette. Roulette game where there is only one green zero on the wheel, instead of the American style of a green zero and green double zero. Because the zeros are the source of the house percentage, European-style roulette charges the player half the house percentage that American-style roulette does on most bets, and still less than that on even-money bets like red, black, 1-18, 19-36, Odd, or Even, because of the "Capture" feature where, if you've made an even money bet, the European-style game leaves your chips in play for another roll, where you can then win or lose it. The capture feature cuts the house percentage in half yet again, making the game quite fair, as casino games go.

Fear/Greed Index. An individual's balance between the desire to win lots of money and the fear of losing. Varies dramatically from individual to individual, and also changes dramatically after a person has been drinking.

Fish. Gaming term for a weak player. Although usually it refers to someone who is just a bad player, it is also used to refer to weakest player in a given game. Thus, a strong poker player, sitting down with seven world championship-class poker players, would be the fish in the game, even though the strong player might outclass many other fields. In games such as poker, backgammon, bridge, or gin, remember the saying, "If you don't know who the fish in the game is, it's you."

Fluctuations. Random ebb and flow of numbers that create winning and losing streaks. Fluctuations create two huge dangers for gamblers. The first is that a random losing fluctuation might wipe out a gambler's bankroll before he or she has a chance to enjoy some success. The second is that the gambler might observe the fluctuation and believe that there is a reason for it (if red came up three times in a row on a roulette wheel, for example), and then make an unreasonably large bet on the assumption that the fluctuation will continue.

Fold. In poker, to quit a given hand, *gently* tossing your cards towards the dealer. Most poker players would have more winning sessions if they folded more often.

Freebies. Non-gaming term for casino comps.

Gambler's Anonymous. Leading organization for problem gamblers. The phone number to its service office is 1-800-GAMBLER. The nation's leading private expert on compulsive gambling and related addictions is Arnie Wexler of Arnie & Sheila Wexler Associates. His company provides training, consultation to groups (including casinos), and treatment services. He can be reached at 908-774-0019.

Green Chips. $25 chips.

Grind Effect. The extremely important concept that small house percentages, which are relatively unimportant when a player is making just one or two bets, eventually grind the player's bankroll down to nothing, by constantly diminishing the bankroll a little bit at a time.

Hedge. To reduce your risk (and in turn your profit) in a gambling situation by betting against yourself. See the definition of "equity" for one example. Taking insurance in blackjack when you have a blackjack yourself is a hedge—certainly you don't want the dealer to have blackjack, so when you make an insurance bet, you're in effect betting against yourself, or at least against your best interests. Instead of "risking it all" on the dealer's hole card, and either winning 1.5 times your original bet or winning nothing (tying), the insurance bettor hedges by accepting even money. This might make sense if you are usually a $5 bettor who has suddenly made a once-in-a-lifetime $500 bet; $750 is a lot to risk on one card. But the odds are bad: Insurance pays 2-1 but fair payment would be 9-4. So hedging in this manner on a comfortable-sized bet will cost you money, in the long run—yet another reason to stick with bets of a size with which you're comfortable.

High Roller. Someone who makes large bets and/or flashes a very large bankroll. Despite the word "roller," the phrase applies to players of all casino games, not just craps.

Hijacking. Robbery of the players at a private game (usually poker) by an outsider who finds out about all the cash sitting around. Although quite rare, it's no fun, and yet another reason to favor casino gambling over private gambling.

Hit. In blackjack, to take another card. Although movies and television have created the impression that using the phrase "hit me" is the right way to ask for another card, in reality no professional casino will allow you to ask for a card verbally. You can say the words if you like, but you must also use some kind of hand gesture, either pointing at the cards (in a game where both player cards are dealt face-up), or scraping the cards towards you (in a game where the cards are dealt for you to pick up). This rule eliminates arguments about what was or was not said, and allows the unseen overhead casino personnel and video cameras to settle debates.

House Percentage. The amount of each casino player bet that the casino will win in the long run. For any one given bet, the house does not win this percentage of your money; you either win the bet, or lose the bet. In this case, the house percentage is an expression of how likely you are to win or lose that one bet. For example, if you were playing a game with a house percentage of 10 percent, the House would be a 55-45 favorite to win any one given bet.

Inside Straight. A poker hand comprised of a split series of cards, for example, 6, 7, 9, 10. Called an "inside" straight because only one card (in this case an 8) will complete the sequence. Compare this to an "open-ended" straight draw such as 6, 7, 8, 9, where either a 5 or a 10 will give the player a straight.

Keno. Lottery-like game where 80 numbered Ping-Pong balls are blown about in a plastic sphere and 20 are randomly selected as game winners. Huge house percentages make this game a very bad percentage gamble and most players participate only to kill time while waiting for food in casino restaurants.

Kirk, Captain James T. Bold captain of Starship Enterprise whose weekly triumphs over million-to-one odds helped create confusion among viewing public as to the difficulty of winning against million-to-one odds.

Las Vegas Advisor. Excellent newsletter for frequent Las Vegas visitors, collecting in one place information about new deals from casinos, tournaments, and bargains. To inquire about subscribing, call them at (702) 252-0655.

Liberal Slots. Loose Slots.

Long March. Andy Glazer term for walking from casino to casino, leaving each casino after winning or losing a predetermined sum. The idea is to keep any one session or casino from hurting you too badly, and to force natural breaks in the action.

Loose Slots. Casino term for slots that supposedly are set to return a high percentage of the player's investment. Not always the case.

Loss Limiter. Andy Glazer term for a casual gambler who sets a loss limit, rather than saying, "I brought $300 to lose."

MacLeod, Duncan. Highly ethical, quasi-immortal *Highlander* character ("quasi" because he can be killed by having his head cut off with a sword, or by having his television series canceled) who conceivably might live long enough to have a decent chance to win a lottery, although he has only rarely been observed gambling in the show.

Martingale System. A horrible betting system wherein the player continues to double his or her bet after each loss. Doomed to failure because eventually the player has a long losing streak where the house limit prevents the next bet.

Martinizing. Andy Glazer term for a gambler whose faith in his or her system causes him or her to keep playing long after a non-system player would have given up.

Max Coins. The maximum number of coins permitted to be bet on any given slot machine. For the vast majority of machines it is very important to play max coins. If doing so runs you out of money too quickly, you should continue to play max coins, but do so on a lower denomination slot (switch from dollar slots to quarter slots).

Misery Indifference. Extremely dangerous point in a gaming session when the player has lost so much money that he or she is numb from the pain. At this moment, additional losses seem meaningless, and a big loss can suddenly turn into a monumental one.

Money Management. Critically important gaming concept wherein you make bets of a reasonable size, relative to the size of your gaming bankroll. In a broader sense, it also involves the length of time you gamble.

Money Wheel. Also sometimes called "Wheel of Fortune." Terrible odds game designed to attract novice gamblers who are intimidated by the more complicated-looking casino games.

Nickel. $500. Why not just say five hundred? Sometimes gamblers prefer that the non-gamblers around don't know how much they're betting.

Odds Bet. Craps bet that can be made in association with a Pass, Don't Pass, Come, or Don't Come bet. You place your odds bet on the table just behind the Pass Line or just to the side of your Don't Pass bet; for Come and Don't Come bets, give your money to the dealer and tell him/her where you want it. The odds bet is actually a fair bet; the odds the house pays are exactly what the odds of winning or losing are. So the smart player will make a relatively small Pass, Don't Pass, Come or Don't Come bet (where house percentages are eating away your bankroll), and a relatively large odds bet (which is neither favorable or unfavorable) in order to reach the amount of action desired.

One-Armed Bandit. Old term for a slot machine.

Partnership Play. Poker term for cheating by two (or more) partners who enter a game planning on splitting their winnings and losses evenly, and who then make bets and raises calculated to drive non-partners out of pots.

Pass or Pass Line Bet. Craps bet where the player wins if the shooter rolls 7 or 11 on the first (come out) roll, and loses if the shooter rolls 2, 3, or 12. If the shooter rolls any of the other numbers (4, 5, 6, 8, 9, 10) on the first roll, the Pass bettor wins if the shooter rolls his or her original number (called the Point) a second time before rolling a 7.

Pick Three. State-run lottery game where the player picks three numbers from 0-9 with the hopes of winning $500 on a $1 investment. Unfortunately, the odds against winning Pick Three are not 500 to 1, but 1,000 to 1, making it a horrible 50-percent disadvantage gamble.

Point. In craps, the number the shooter rolls on his or her first roll, other than 7, 11, 2, 3, or 12 (i.e., any 4, 5, 6, 8, 9, or 10).

Pointspread. The handicap allotted by bookmakers to lesser teams, encouraging bettors to risk their money on the underdog. For example, a very powerful football team might be favored by 20 points over a weak team. By offering a 20 point "spread" to bettors, bookies get more equal action on the game, because bettors who bet on the underdog know their team merely has to avoid getting slaughtered for them to win the bet. If you bet the underdog in such a situation and your team loses 37-20, you still win your bet. The pointspread is not so much a bookie's prediction of what will happen in the game, as it as a number that the bookie's experience tells him will create equal interest in both teams (see discussion of *vig* for more on this).

Pot Odds. In poker, the concept that the amount of money already in the pot, or the amount likely to be in the pot at the hand's conclusion, should bear an important relationship to the size of your bet, and whether certain hands are playable. For example, if there is a lot of money in the pot, and you only have to make a small call to try to claim it, it is often worth calling even if the chances of winning aren't very good, because the amount you are risking with the final call is very small, relative to what you stand to win.

Progressive Slot Machine. A machine whose jackpot is constantly increasing, because a tiny percentage of each coin played is withheld to add to the jackpot. After someone wins the jackpot, the machine resets the progressive jackpot to a much lower starting number. Players should avoid progressive machines that have just been hit recently and look for machines whose jackpots have built up high.

Pyramid Scheme. Monumentally stupid, illegal form of gambling where you speculate by putting money into the scheme, and then hope that:

1. Neither you nor the scheme organizer gets arrested.
2. The scheme doesn't collapse before you get paid (extremely likely, since collapse is absolutely inevitable).
3. When the scheme collapses, the friends you brought in don't lose their money and never talk to you again.

Rake. Also called *House Rake*. Mostly a poker term, the rake is the amount literally raked, or dragged, out of each pot by the dealer and collected for the house. It is usually expressed or advertised by the casino as a percentage ("10-percent max rake") of each pot taken, against a maximum figure (so that if the pot gets very large, the casino isn't taking a huge chunk of it). A rake is used in lower stakes poker games; in higher stakes games, the players usually pay "Time" for their seats, with the house collecting a set sum, usually a little less than half of one minimum bet (for example $7 in a 15-30 game) every half-hour. Although House Rakes or paying Time make it more difficult to beat a poker game over the long run, players get one significant compensation—the house isn't trying to beat them. All the house wants is a table full of players; whoever wins isn't important. So you don't have to be better than the casino to win at casino poker: you just have to be better than the other players, who are people like you, with their own individual strengths, weaknesses, intellects, and emotions.

Random Number Generator. Also called RNG. A computer microprocessor component of virtually all modern slot machines, the RNG constantly generates random numbers that correspond to stopping points on the slot reels you see. The trick is, you see the symbols on the reels, but not necessarily the stopping points, so while it might look like you have a 1-in-20 chance of having the jackpot symbol come up on a reel, it might be as much as a one-in-256 chance. The RNG plays a big role in the psychological/emotional aspects of playing the slots, too. It is spitting out new random combinations every millisecond, so if you get up from playing a slot for two hours, and a new player hits the jackpot on his or her first pull, try not to get upset—the new player didn't win the jackpot that you would have won if you stayed just a few moments longer. The new player just happened to pull the lever at the right split-second, something that you didn't do in two hours and might not have done if you'd stayed there for a month. Intellectually, most players can accept this, but psychologically it's a little tougher. If you're prone to agonize about things you have no control over, I suggest that when you finish playing a slot, go far enough away so that you can't see what happens to the machine next.

Rated (Getting). Having the casino evaluate both the size of your average bet and the length of time you play per day, in order to qualify for comps. Makes moving from casino to casino virtually impossible, and moving from table to table within a casino a hassle, because with each move you need to notify a floorperson that you are a rated player.

Rated Player. Someone who lets the casino know his or her identity each time he or she begins play, so the casino can track bet size and length of play, for awarding comps. If a rated player visits the same casino frequently, or makes one very long visit, eventually the casino personnel come to know and recognize him or her, making it somewhat easier for the player to move from table to table. Well-known players are often greeted by their last initial, as in, "Nice to see you, Mr. G."

Rat-holing. A very desirable system of stashing some chips away when you are winning, so that when the winning streak ends, you still have something positive to show for it.

RNG. *See* Random Number Generator.

Rope-a-dope. Boxing style used by Muhammed Ali, which entailed leaning back onto the ropes, letting his opponents hit him repeatedly, and then attacking when they tired. Not a viable strategy when the opponent is a casino that does not get tired.

Rush. Two usages. One involves a physical or emotional thrill, a feeling of great excitement; for some people, the mere act of gambling generates this kind of rush, while for others, only winning generates it. A second definition comes from the poker world, where "rush" is used as a synonym for "hot streak." You will frequently hear poker players defend bad calls by claiming they were "playing their rush." This meant they felt they were on a hot streak and wanted to keep playing even though the odds indicated that they should have folded their hand.

Session Betting. Andy Glazer term for playing until you have won or lost a set predetermined amount, and then leaving the casino or taking a break.

Shill. A player who works for the House for a variety of reasons, the most common being to help start a game. (Many players don't like walking up to an empty table, but will gladly join in the action if one person is already playing.)

Shooter. In a craps game, the player rolling the dice. No skill is required to do this other than enough strength to roll the dice far enough to hit the back wall of the craps table.

Slot Club. A casino's system for tracking how much slot action the player is giving the house, and in turn rewarding the player with a set number of slot club points. These points can be redeemed for merchandise and/or discounts on rooms, meals, or even airfare reimbursement.

Small Bank Progressive Slot Machine. A small group of slot machines tied together to build a larger progressive jackpot than an individual progressive machine could achieve, but much smaller than a wide area progressive.

Soft Hand. In blackjack, a hand that includes an Ace that cannot be busted by taking a card. For example, Ace-5 is "soft 16," not nearly as bad a hand as 10-6, even though they are both 16. With 10-6, drawing any card greater than a 5 will bust your hand, and you lose; with Ace-5, because of the dual nature of the Ace as either a 1 or an 11, you get *two* chances to draw a good card. You can either draw an Ace, 2, 3, 4, or 5 right away, giving you a hand in the 17-21 range; or if you draw a higher card (6 through 10), you have a *stiff* hand, which you can hit again (against a strong dealer upcard), or stand on (against a weak dealer upcard). Soft hands provide you with a free shot at the dealer. Standing on a hand like Ace-4 is a terrible play because you have a chance to improve, and are taking no risk at all by hitting; even if you get a 10, you still have a total of 15, and you can stand then.

Sort of Big Score. A reasonably large gambling win, very enjoyable, but not quite enough to make a big difference in life-style. That the acronym for "Sort of Big Score" is SOBS is just a coincidence.

Stand. In blackjack, the player's decision to take no additional cards. The dealer has no choice about standing; he or she must take a card if he or she has 16 or less, and must stand if he or she has 17 or more. In some casinos, the dealer must hit soft 17 (Ace-6), which is a slightly dealer-favorable rule. Although movies and television have created the impression that using the phrase "I'm good" is the right way to stand, in reality no professional casino will allow you to play your hand verbally. *See the discussion of "Hit" for the casino's rationale.*

Stick. Identical to *Stand,* above.

Stickman. In craps, the dealer who uses the wooden rattan stick to collect the dice after a roll and push them back to the shooter. The stickman controls the pace of the game, and if doing his or her job correctly, doesn't return the dice to the shooter until all existing wagers have been settled and all players have had a reasonable length of time to make new bets.

Stiff. In blackjack, a hand that can be busted by one card. Any hand 12 or higher is a stiff, although because players never hit hands of 17 or higher, usually people just refer to the hands 12-16 as the stiff hands.

Stinger. Andy Glazer term for a player who employs the "float like a butterfly, sting like a bee" style of play, playing for a little while and then pulling back either to enjoy the taste of victory or clear his/her head from the troubles of defeat.

Stud. A kind of poker game (usually 5-Card Stud or 7-Card Stud), where some of each player's own cards are turned face up for his opponents to see, as opposed to Draw Poker, where a player's entire hand is concealed.

System. A scheme for playing a game according to a particular pattern of play. Usually systems have no effect, positive or negative, on the expected results of a casino game, and so are harmless in and of themselves. But they become very dangerous if the player's belief in the system causes him or her to continue playing (and losing) long after a non-system player would have quit. If someone offers to sell you a system, consider why they are willing to sell it: If the system were really that good, wouldn't they be using it themselves?

TANSTAAFL: Author Robert Heinlein's acronym for *There Ain't No Such Thing As A Free Lunch,* meaning that if a casino is willing to give you something that appears to be free, there is probably a very good and costly reason why it is willing to do so.

TEF. The Entertainment Formula. Andy Glazer term for holding your gambling losses to an amount equivalent to what you would spend on other forms of entertainment.

Texas Hold 'Em. Often just called Hold 'Em. Popular poker game where each player is dealt two cards of his own, followed by a round of betting. Three cards that belong to all the players at the table (called community cards) are then turned face up in the middle (this is called "the flop"), followed by another round of betting. A fourth community card is then turned up (called "the turn"), followed by another round of betting, and then a fifth and final community card (called "the river") is turned up, followed by the final bet. Each player can thus make use of the two cards of his or her own and any or all of the five community cards to make a hand. Because so many of the cards are exposed, it is much easier to guess what an opponent might have than in most other poker games.

Vig or Vigorish. Two usages. The more general usage means any little extra edge or advantage in any form of gambling. For example, someone might say, "I had a nice little vig in that blackjack game because I could see the dealer's hole card sometimes." The more specific usage refers to the commission (usually 10 percent) charged by bookmakers or casino Sports Books on losing wagers. This, rather than poor selections, is the main source of house profit on sports bets. For a bookie, ideal customer betting action would be equal on both teams, say, for example, $10,000 on Dallas and $10,000 on Green Bay. Whoever won, the bookie would collect $11,000 from the losers and pay $10,000 to the winners, thus profiting by $1,000 without worry about the game result. When a major sports upset occurs, many non-gaming experts tend to think this means the bookies "took a beating." Actually the opposite is more likely true. Most sports bettors tend to bet on favored teams, meaning that when an underdog springs an upset, usually the bookie does very well.

Wide Area Progressive. Slot machine that, because of inter-linking with thousands of identical machines in other casinos, offers a huge jackpot.

World Series of Poker. Huge, $10,000 entry fee Texas Hold 'Em poker tournament held annually at Binion's in Las Vegas. The winner of the million-dollar prize is considered the World Poker Champion. People who don't have $10,000 to invest in an entry fee can try to win entry by winning a "satellite" tournament (a $1,000 entry fee tournament where 10 players sit down at a table and the winner gains entry to the main tournament) or a "supersatellite" tournament with still more entrants (for example, a $100 entry fee and 100 entrants), out of which one person will emerge with an entry into the main draw of the tournament. The presence of satellite and supersatellite winners in the World Series is one of the main attractions to the poker pros willing to put up $10,000 to win, since amateur players, although capable of getting lucky for a while, rarely possess the kind of skill and experience necessary to go all the way and win the big tournament.

Index

A

Action, definition, 231
Albee, Edward Francis, 181, 184
Ali, Muhammed, 25
All-Star games, 1992, 196, 199
Andy's Enlightened Casino, 203-206, 231
Atlantic City, 97, 98, 121, 122, 124

B

Baccarat, 164, 234
Backgammon, 159-160
Bahamas, 33, 34, 159
Bankroll, 231
Basic strategy, 231
Biased roulette wheel, 231
Big Chill, The, 69
Big Score, The, 103, 106, 107-111, 139, 185, 231
Big Six/Big Eight bet, 39, 231
Binion's Horseshoe, 110
Black chips, 232
Blackjack Blitz, 156
Blackjack, 91, 131, 155-158, 163, 166, 193, 203
basic strategy, 156-158, 163
bust, 232
card counter, 232
dealer, 157
double down, 235
simplified strategy, 225-227, 229-230
tournament, 187
Bookie, 196
Boom-Boom strategy, 207-210, 232
Boom-Boom-Boom strategy, 209, 210, 232
Boxman, dealer, 174
Break points, slots, 149
Bust, 232
Bust out, definition, 232

C

Caddyshack, 234
Call, 232
Card counter, 232
Caribbean Stud, 191, 192
Casino tournaments, 109, 185-189, 233
blackjack, 187
slots, 188
two types, 186-187

Casinos,
  as opponents, 165-167
  cheating, 171-172
  foreign countries, 167
Cheating, 171-174, 216
  by fellow players, 175-180
  casinos, 171-172
  dealers, 172-174
  partnership play, 177-179
  poker, 177-180
  slots, 176-177
Checks, 233
Chip coppers, 176
Chips, 233
  black, 232
  green, 237
Come bet, 174, 233
Come out, 233
Comps, 167, 233
  at casinos, 114-115
  gambling mistakes, 217
  RFB, 115
  slot, 115-116
Cramden, Ralph, 234
Craps, 54, 90, 91, 163-164,
  167, 172, 181-184, 204,
  207-208
Crapspeak, 30, 52, 234
Croupier, 29, 234
Croupier, 29

D
Dance of the living dead,
  175, 179, 234

Day, Laura, 132
Dealer,
  blackjack, 157
  boxman, 174
  cheating, 172-174
  impressing, 30-31
Dependent streaks, 60, 61,
  62
Dime, 235
Dodge, get out of, 235
Don't Come bet, 235
Don't Pass bet, 54, 235
Double down, 235
Drinking, and gambling,
  113-114, 216, 218
Drop, 148, 235

E
Entertainment Formula,
  The, 118-120
Equity, 235
Esalen Institute, 203, 236
ESPN, 199
Even money, 61, 151

F
F-Troop, 116
Fear/greed index, 236-237
Field bet, 38, 163, 192, 204
Fields, W. C., 181, 184
Fish, 237
Float like a butterfly, 25,
  26, 27, 28, 98
Fluctuations, 237

Fold, 237
Foreman, George, 25, 26, 27
Freebies, 237

G
Gambler's Anonymous, 96, 237
Gambler, The, 157
Gambling vacations, 33-35
Gambling,
  as a profession, 212
  as entertainment, 117-120
  10 Basic Rules, 215-216
  10 mistakes, 217-219
Green chips, 237
Grind effect, 88, 89, 163, 237

H
Hardway bet, 38, 39, 161, 162, 163-164, 192, 204
Hedge, 238
High roller, 238
Hijacking, 171, 238
Hit, 238
Hitchhiker's Guide to the Galaxy, 151
House percentages, 89. 90, 131, 146, 171, 183, 192, 239

I
Independent streaks, 60, 61, 62
Inside straight, poker, 239
Instruction, to gambling, 21
Intuition, 131-134

J
Jackpots, 138, 143, 149
  cheating, 177
Jeopardy, 61

K
Keno, 95, 108, 239
Kirk, Captain James T., 239
Klink, Colonel, 56, 57, 58

L
Lake Tahoe, 33
Las Vegas Advisor, 108-109, 156, 167, 239
Las Vegas Vacation, 194
Las Vegas, 33, 35, 97, 98, 100, 121, 122, 124, 129, 168, 204
Laws of probability, 131
Liberal slots, 239
Limit, poker, 169
Long March, 28, 239
Loose slots, 239
Loss limiter, 39, 240
Lost in America, 129

Lottery, 103-106
  California, 104
Luck, 159-164, 216
  gambling mistakes, 219

M
MacLeod, Duncan, 240
Marino, Dan, 195, 196
Martingale system, 47-50, 240
Martinizing, 53, 240
Maximum coins, slots, 138, 142, 240
Megabucks, 108, 139
Misery indifference, 80, 81, 219, 240
Money management, 183, 218, 240
  gambling advice, 151-154
Money wheel, 240
Motivation, for gambling, 93-96

N
Nickel, 241
No Limit, poker, 169

O
Octopussy, 64
Odds bet, 182, 241
10x odds, 183, 194
100x odds, 167, 183, 194, 231

One-armed bandit, 241
Opponents, 165-169
  casinos, 165-167
  individuals, 168-169
Optimist March, 28
Over-Under bet, sports betting, 199

P
Partnership play, cheating, 177-179, 241
Pass Line bet, 54, 91, 39, 90, 161, 162, 181, 182, 204, 209, 241
Pick Three, 241
Pickpockets, 175
Point, 241
Pointspread, 73, 197, 242
Poker, 132, 168, 169
  cheating, 177-180
  inside straight, 239
Pot Limit, poker, 169
Pot Odds, 242
Practical Intuition for Success, 132
Practical Intuition, 132
Professional Gambler's Paradox, 211-214
Progressive slot machine, 139, 143, 242
Pyramid scheme, 55, 56, 242

R
Rake, 243
Random number
generators (RNGs), 142,
142, 243, 244
Rat-holing, 110, 244
Rated, getting, 244
Rated player, 244
Rationalizing, 69-72
Records, keeping, 153
Reno/Tahoe, 124
Resorts, in Atlantic City,
121
RFB comps, 115
Risk-tolerance, test for, 75
Rocky, 185
Romancing the Stone, 186
Rope-a-dope, 25, 26, 244
Roulette, 90, 164, 167, 172
biased wheel, 231
croupier, 234
European style, 236
Rush, 244

S
Seat-selling, 145
Session betting, 87, 245
Shill, 22, 245
Simplified Blackjack
Strategy, 156, 158, 225-
227, 229-230
Slot club, 245
Slots, 44, 91, 108, 137-140,
141-146, 147-150, 163,
167

casino tournaments, 188
cheating, 176-177
drop, 148
jackpots, 138
maximum coins, 138
progressive slot machine,
242
progressive, 139, 143
Small bank progressive
slot machine, 245
Soft hand, 245
Sort of Big Score, 246
Spanish 21, 191, 192
Sports betting, 195-200
Sports Book, bookie, 196
Stand, 246
*Star Trek VI, The
Undiscovered Country,*
132
Stick, 246
Stickman, 246
Stiff, 246
Stinger, 246
Streaks,
dependent, 60, 61, 62
independent, 60, 61, 62
winning, 59-65, 214
Stud, 247
Sugar Bowl game, 1982,
195
System, 47-65, 247

T
Table games, 191-194
Taking a shot, 185-186

TANSTAAFL, 116, 247
TEF, 118-120, 247
Texas Hold 'Em, 178, 247

V
Vacations, gambling, 33-35
Video blackjack, 156
Video poker, 141-149, 150
Vigorish (vig), 196, 197, 200, 248

W
War, card game, 191-192, 194
Web site, 18, 19
Wide area progressive, 108, 109, 248
Winning streaks, 59-65, 214
World According to Garp, The, 59
World Series of Poker, 178, 179, 248
World Team Backgammon Championships, 1984, 159-160